Cities of the World:

LENINGRAD

Also in this series

ATHENS	Kevin Andrews
BANGKOK	James Kirkup
BARCELONA	Clifford King
BRUSSELS	K. M. Willcox
CAIRO	Desmond Stewart
HONG KONG	James Kirkup
ISTANBUL	Peter Mayne
JERUSALEM	Stewart Perowne
MUNICH	Egon Larsen
PARIS	Alexander Reid
VIENNA	Christa Esterházy

Cities of the World:

LENINGRAD

WRIGHT MILLER

With 20 photographs and 2 maps

A. S. BARNES AND COMPANY

South Brunswick and New York

© Text, Wright Miller 1970

All rights reserved

Printed in Great Britain
by
Cox & Wyman Ltd.
London, Fakenham and Reading
for
A. S. BARNES AND CO. INC.
Cranbury, N. J. 08512
by arrangements with
J. M. DENT & SON LTD
Aldine House . Bedford Street . London

First published 1970

Library of Congress Catalog Card No. 72–101214

By the same author:

THE YOUNG TRAVELLER IN RUSSIA

RUSSIANS AS PEOPLE

RUSSIA – A PERSONAL ANTHOLOGY

THE U.S.S.R.

Contents

List of Illustrations and Maps,   vii

1   Peter's City   1

2   The Empresses   18

3   Repression, Reform and Revolution   32

4   Leningrad Today   59

    Index   78

List of Illustrations

Between pages 20 and 21

Plan of St Petersburg in 1753—Hare Island in the centre.

The Hermitage and Winter Palace seen across the Neva. *John Massey Stewart, from 'Across the Russias', by courtesy of the Harvill Press*

Palace Square with Rossi's General Staff Building and the Alexander Column, the tallest granite column in the world. *John Massey Stewart, from 'Across the Russias', by courtesy of the Harvill Press*

The old Admiralty, the central point of Leningrad's city plan. *Novosti Agency*

A White Night on the Griboyedov Canal, with the Church of the Saviour 'on the Blood'. *John Massey Stewart, from 'Across the Russias', by courtesy of the Harvill Press.*

Spring on the Neva, opposite the fortress and Cathedral of St Peter and St Paul. *Novosti Agency*

One of the rostral columns commemorating naval victories. *Novosti Agency*

Smolny, the Leningrad headquarters of the Communist Party. *Novosti Agency*

The 'Kunstkamer' or Anthropological Museum. *D. M. Gregory-Jones, A.R.I.B.A.*

Between pages 52 and 53

A life-size figure of Peter the Great in the Hermitage Museum. *John Massey Stewart, from 'Across the Russias', by courtesy of the Harvill Press*

The Winter Palace, now part of the Hermitage Museum. *Novosti Agency*

The main staircase inside the Hermitage. *John Massey Stewart, from 'Across the Russias', by courtesy of the Harvill Press*
Natasha Kuchinskaya, a Soviet champion in gymnastics
A patrol of workers during the siege of Leningrad
Russian visitors to Lenin's room in the Smolny
On a quayside in Leningrad. *John Massey Stewart, from 'Across the Russias', by courtesy of the Harvill Press*
'The Bronze Horseman'—Peter the Great—Leningrad's finest statue. *F. R. Yerbury, from the Architectural Association's collection.*
The Cameron Gallery of Catherine the Great's Palace at Tsarskoe Selo. *Novosti Agency*
The cascades and palace at Peterhof. *Katharine Miller*
The 'Upper Bath House' by the lake at Tsarskoe Selo. *John Massey Stewart, from 'Across the Russias', by courtesy of the Harvill Press*

MAPS by Katharine Miller, pages x–xi and 24

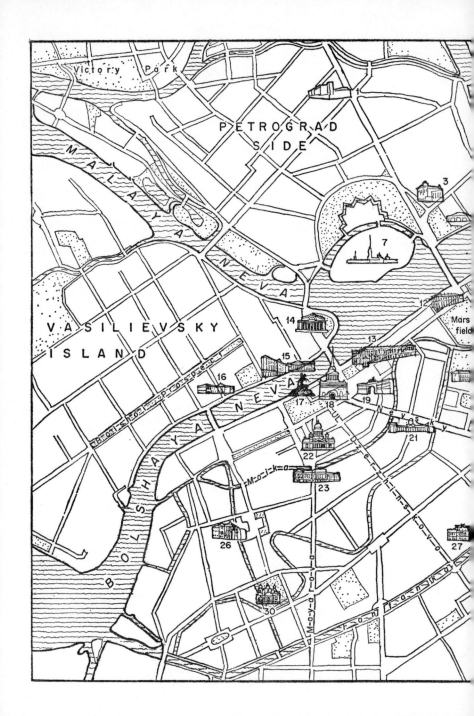

Chapter 1

Peter's City

EVERY time I arrive in Leningrad from Moscow I feel that I am somehow returning to Europe. This may be partly the effect of the station itself, which is high-arched and a little like St Pancras in its interior, and partly because of the city, the old capital, the most European city in Russia, which I know is waiting for me outside. You walk straight down the steps on to the Nevsky Prospect, you look along more than two miles of it to the glittering spire of the Admiralty, and you know that every yard of that two miles is worth walking—for history, for architectural beauty or distinction, for the exhilaration of modern life, or for all three.

But as I walk down the platform I feel at the same time that I am walking through the scene of so many occasions in the great Russian novels, the station of bitter partings and rapturous welcomes, the station where Anna Karenina said good-bye to her husband, and I look to see whether perhaps there is not some stiff Karenin or gallant Vronsky waiting to welcome some Anna of our own day. Or out on the Nevsky too one could believe they must be standing somewhere, aloof from the crowds. In the evening I shall go to the ballet in the Marinsky Theatre, where Pavlova and Karsavina made their reputations, dancing before the Tsar. . . .

This is not just the sentimentalizing of a foreigner. The dual impression of classical Russia and yet of Europe makes something which Russians themselves feel and have always felt about the city on the Neva. A descendant of an old Russian family, Henri Troyat, says: 'No Russian was ever out of his element when he arrived in Moscow for the first time, but everyone was so when arriving for the first time in St Petersburg. They did not feel at home, though they felt to some extent in Europe.'

It is the city of Tchaikovsky and Dostoevsky, of Pushkin's fatal duel, of Diaghilev and the Imperial Ballet, of the hierarchies and drilled magnificence of the Imperial Court, of the Imperial Academy of Sciences and Mendeleyev's Periodic Table of Elements, of underground plottings and assassinations of Tsars, of three great Revolutions and of Lenin. It is the background to at least three-quarters of what most foreigners know about Russia, and yet it is a city planned, in a most un-Russian way; it is classical and colonnaded and its tallest tips are gilt; it has very few of the tumbling onion domes and gaudy brickwork that are typically Russian; it has no Russian untidiness, no grass-grown corners or little alleyways; it is dignified and aristocratic without any of the dominating mass of the Kremlin. In all its significance and history it is Russian and yet as a city it isn't just Russian, though one would be hard put to it to say where else it might be. It is Leningrad–St Petersburg.

It has only been Leningrad since 1924. It was Petrograd for only ten years before that, and St Petersburg itself only began to rise out of the mists and marshes in 1703. And yet it has not the appearance of a new or even a modern city—except in the great southern suburbs built since the war, and even here the banality of Soviet taste seems to have benefited from the intervention of the Leningrad city architect, or the Leningrad City Soviet, the same authorities, whoever they may be, who have always resisted any proposal to introduce either tall concrete blocks or Stalinist wedding-cakes into the city laid down by Peter and Elizabeth and Catherine. Leningrad remains as stylized and yet perennial in appearance as the best parts of Bath or Edinburgh's New Town or rebuilt Dresden; it is grander than any of them, of course, a great deal vaster, and also more lively. Only sometimes, on the huge embankments and opensided squares of pink granite, by the Hermitage or the giant bronze figure of Peter the Great, does

one feel that the distances are too Versailles-like for a city which
is to be lived in. Anywhere else—in the courtyards round the
fortress of St Peter and St Paul, by the lovely canals, among the
statues under the trees of the Summer Garden, in the avenues with
their crawling strings of yellow trams, and above all in the Nevsky
Prospect, where everyone promenades or shops—it is a city which
is grandiose but which still manages to remain on a human scale.
This is rather a remarkable achievement on a site so monoton-
ously flat. Modern Leningrad covers at least three times the area
of St Petersburg, and its great thoroughfares still stretch away
into a dead-level distance with no natural vistas other than the
pearly sky. Yet the buildings are not quite dwarfed by the distance, nor are they oppressively tall—five storeys is about the
average in the old city. The blocks are not all set to a uniform
building line either, but are frequently recessed. The Nevsky
Prospect is forty yards across through almost its whole length
and is not planted with trees, but its skyline is of such a modestly
varying height, and the frontages are so changing in design, that
as one strolls along the broad pavement one feels that one is
comfortably 'in' the Nevsky as in an elongated precinct; in spite of
the great vista down the middle it doesn't seem an avenue in two
halves, like the Champs–Elysées.

The canals, unlike those of Venice, have embankments, usually
on both sides, to walk or drive along; the old palaces were hardly
ever built to the water's edge, and most of the frontages are not
in fact noble mansions but old apartment blocks more reminiscent
of a *haute bourgeoisie*. Professors and technologists, teachers and
ship's officers and theatre people share them today with more
rank-and-file workers, but probably on the whole they are ten-
anted by people whom we would call middle class by occupation
—people who will put up with old-fashioned inconvenience and
dark passages for the sake of the position on the canal. It is all
much more spacious than Amsterdam, though Peter had Amsterdam in mind when he founded the city. It is less intimate; all the

footways by the canals have stout old pre-revolutionary railings instead of being open to the water's edge in the Dutch manner. St Petersburg was rarely, I think, called 'the Amsterdam of the North'. Sometimes it was 'the Northern Venice', but most often it was 'the Palmyra of the North', a title which mystified me until I remembered the eighteenth-century way of regarding certain kinds of landscape. It was 'Palmyra' because of its classical and luxurious majesty, and Palmyra rather than any other classical city because it was erected, like the luxurious Syrian Palmyra, in the midst of what, in the romantic terminology of our ancestors, amounts to 'a desert'.

The mouth of the Neva was indeed a most unpromising site for a capital city. Inhabited only by a few fishermen, it was—and still is where it has not been built on—a waste of brackish sedge and bitter tussocky marsh seamed with ditches, enlivened by nothing more in nature than the white tufts of cottongrass and sparse yellow hawkweed, with rare straggling birch and fir trees.

But then Peter did not begin with the intention of founding a capital. From 1700 to 1721 he fought the Great Northern War against Sweden, to win undisputed possession at last of that outlet to the Baltic for which Russia had fought during seven centuries against the Swedes, the Germans and the Poles. The southern shore of the Gulf of Finland, and across to Lake Ladoga, was Ingria, which the Swedes called Ingermanland, and the Russians the land of the Izhory, a Finnish people who paid tribute in the Middle Ages to the powerful commercial city of Novgorod. They became Russianized and they provided Novgorod with an access to the sea for her considerable western trade. But Ingria was lost in the seventeenth century, and Russia was left with Archangel as her only port.

The young Peter joined in an alliance against Sweden which at first met with unexpected and ignominious defeat. His whole army of 40,000 men was completely routed in 1700 outside Narva, on the Estonian border, by a much smaller force under

Charles XII, who attacked in a raging snowstorm. Charles was only eighteen at the time, and his victory was the first of many which made him the most magnetic general of his age. Peter, however, was not only a magnetic and towering leader, he was also tenacious, and he was an overwhelming and many-sided organizer. He imposed levy after levy of men, money and supplies on his people, adding about 30,000 men a year to his army. (They were recruited selectively, so as not to disrupt agriculture.) He set up new arms and powder factories in the Urals, he produced more and more artillery as well as small arms, and he spent about 80 per cent of his budget on military preparations. Not that a budget of the early 1700s can be interpreted in the same way as the budget of a modern State: there were few heads of civil expenditure, Peter had little taste for personal spending or show, and when revenue ran short he slapped on fresh requisitions and confiscations. Quite early on he confiscated the whole income of the estates of the Church. He had already paid his first visit abroad, and in 1702 he invited 'all qualified foreigners' to Russia, all technically or professionally qualified foreigners 'except Jews', promising them their own courts and religious freedom when they got there, besides secure and well-paid employment. By this means he vastly increased the stream of Dutch, English, Scottish, German, French, Italian and Danish artillery experts, instrument-makers, architects, gardeners, adventurers, artists, musicians, and merchants, who settled in Russia for long periods or for good, and who played a fundamental part in Westernizing the country—on the surface at least—all through the century.

By 1702 Peter felt strong enough to attack Ingria again. The Swedes had strong positions at each end of the River Neva, and he first seized one on Lake Ladoga, where the Neva begins its course, and gave it the German name of Schlüsselburg, because it was 'the key' to the Karelian isthmus. (Under Soviet rule it has at last acquired a Russian name: it is now Petrokrepost, or 'Peter's Fort'.) At the mouth of the Neva, on the right bank where it is

joined by the River Okhta, was the other Swedish fort, Nyenskans, which was already a trading centre. On 1st May 1703 Peter
forced it to surrender, and a fortnight later he turned the first
sods of a new earthwork on an island a little farther downstream,
in the delta of the Neva—Hare Island, as the Finns called it. He
cut the first two sods with a bayonet, laid them crosswise, saying
'Here shall be a town', and buried a casket containing relics of St
Andrew and some gold coins. The hexagonal fort of clay and
wood was later replaced by a brick structure with six bastions,
after plans by the French engineer Lambert, a pupil of the great
Vauban. Catherine II faced it with pink granite, and that is the
fortress of St Peter and St Paul which exists today.

Hare Island was thus the nucleus of St Petersburg, and the
400-foot gilded needle of its old cathedral still indicates the centre
of the city—a delicate, beautiful landmark across six hundred
yards of the Neva from the Winter Palace, or from the bridges, or
from almost any vantage-point in Leningrad. It is an extremely
un-Russian building, though some imitations of it were built later,
both in St Petersburg and elsewhere. In 1714 it was a deliberate
assertion of one of the most revolutionary aspects of Peter's
break with the past—in this case the Byzantine past of Moscow
with its bulbous domes. The Orthodox Church is a Church of
rigidly traditional customs and ritual; it is laid down that its
churches should have a central dome and four domes at the
corners, in the same style, it is alleged, as the first Christian church
in Jerusalem. Elaborations and ramifications of this theme are
permissible, to a state of fussiness and near chaos indeed, as with
St Basil's in the Red Square, but Peter wanted a clean break away
from all that. He saw to it that his cathedral of St Peter and St
Paul should be externally of a severely Protestant design, resemb-
ling a German or Dutch church. His architect, the Italian–Swiss
Trezzini, had worked for the Danish court and absorbed the
Dutch influence which was then affecting design all over northern,
Protestant Europe. The spire, Peter emphasized, was to be taller

than the great belltower of Ivan the Great in the Kremlin, which
is by far the tallest ecclesiastical building in Moscow. The cathedral was built inside the fortress, and it was here that Peter or-
dained that he was to be buried. (Almost all his successors too
were laid to rest in this Germanic building.) Peter's architectural
innovations scandalized many of the devout, even though the
interior of the cathedral is comparatively Orthodox. Add to this
that he was known to enjoy the company of Lutheran (i.e.
heathen) whores, that he abolished the Patriarchate and that he
gave over all its power, especially its power over Church property,
to the Synod, which he made into a department of State, and it is
not surprising that a rumour went round that Tsar Peter was actually the Antichrist.

Peter's young city was intended in the first place as a point of
defence for his newly won access to the Baltic, and it was to have
as soon as possible, and did have, wharves and a shipyard where
a Russian fleet would be built. Peter sailed one of the first Russian
boats on the Baltic with his own hands; he had learned both
sailing and boat-building as a youth on one of the royal lakes,
with a derelict English sailing boat as a model. In its first year St
Petersburg had a visit from a Dutch merchantman, and in the
following year the first English ship anchored there.

In the first year after the foundation of St Petersburg its position was immensely strengthened by the seizing of a much larger
island nineteen miles down the Gulf of Finland, where the fort
and naval base to be known later as Kronstadt were started up
with the same maniacal petrine speed. The Swedes had made an
unsuccessful attempt on Hare Island within two months of its
first settlement, and they made four more attacks, by sea or by
land, on St Petersburg or on Kronstadt during the next five
years, but all were repulsed. In 1704 Peter captured Narva, the
scene of his defeat four years earlier, but it was not until 1709,
with the routing of Charles XII in the south, at Poltava, that his
Baltic conquests could be considered finally secure. When Peter

heard the news of Poltava he said exultantly: 'Now the final stone is laid on the foundations of St Petersburg.' He thought of his city already as a great trading port and a capital which was to be of European appearance. For defence purposes Kronstadt was a much stronger base, and St Petersburg was never given a ring of walls.

The price in human misery of Peter's haste to build his capital is well known. Soldiers put up the first huts and tents, but by the autumn of 1703, 20,000 peasants, prisoners, vagrants and deserters had been gathered together in the marshes, sleeping mostly in the open, badly fed, digging the earth without any tools but their hands and carrying it in their own garments. The following year Peter stepped up his demands to 40,000 workmen a year from the provinces 'with their tools'. Not until 1718 was it thought more productive to put the building force on a normal hiring basis. (There was a promising source for hiring: serfs who managed to escape from their master's lands into industrial work were safe from recapture.) Work went on through the icy Baltic blasts and fogs and freezings of winter, and through the recurrent floods, which in 1705 covered the whole of the new settlement several feet deep. Thousands of labourers were drowned or died of dysentery, lung diseases or sheer exhaustion. The whole country was laid under tribute, and it was not only serfs and prisoners who were dragooned into building St Petersburg. The erection of stone buildings anywhere else in Russia was forbidden, and everyone entering the city was obliged to bring with him a stone, or if he came in a boat or cart several stones. A few years after the founding all officials, nobles, or landowners who owned thirty or more families of serfs were ordered to come and settle in St Petersburg and build houses for themselves on a scale according to their means; if they owned 500 serfs they had to build a stone house of two storeys, but lesser families had to build wooden houses, some of them 'in the old English style', which were put up hurriedly and became dilapidated before long.

From the very beginning St Petersburg was not confined to Hare Island but spread to the larger island group behind it, where the settlement was known as the Petrograd Side, more than two centuries before the whole city was named Petrograd. Beyond the delta to the north-east, where the way to Finland begins, was the Vyborg Side, later to develop as an industrial and proletarian area. There were settlements and draining on Vasilievsky Ostrov, or Basil's Island, which lies at the great branching of the Neva into the Bolshaya and the Malaya—the Greater and Lesser Neva—and makes the well-known vantage corner where the pillared Bourse and the rostral columns stand to this day. Peter expected his city to expand mostly in these northern districts, but as soon as he founded his Admiralty yard on the south bank the houses began to spread on this more accessible mainland area, and in a few decades the central and grandest part of the city was here, particularly after the Imperial Palaces went up on the great southern embankment of the Neva. Most of what foreigners know about St Petersburg from Russian literature and history is associated with this southern half of the city, known as Great Side or Admiralty Side. The two and three-quarter miles of the Nevsky Prospect were laid down across the marshes from the Admiralty and through the forest in Peter's time, though the buildings which line it today are all of later periods. That is, until one comes, after the bend by the station, to the very end, at the Monastery of Alexander Nevsky which gives the great avenue its name. The relics of the hero and saint who had also defeated the Swedes, almost 500 years earlier, were brought here from Vladimir by Peter's command, to lie in the monastery cathedral which he had built.

Peter himself had so little use for luxury that he lived for eight years in the single-storey log-house, painted to look like Dutch brick, which was the first house to be put up on the Petrograd Side. Catherine the Great enclosed this *domik* in a stone building to protect it, and there it is still to be seen—the oldest edifice in

Leningrad. In 1713 Peter moved into the Summer Palace on the
south bank, at the junction of the Neva and the Fontanka canal.
This is a solid house but remarkably modest to be called a palace;
on each of its two floors it has six living-rooms, a kitchen, a
servants' room, and a corridor—nothing grander. Again in
Dutch style, and designed by Trezzini, it might be a mansion for
some English squire under William and Mary. There was nothing
sentimental about Peter's preference for Dutch architecture. He
favoured it because St Petersburg had swampy foundations, like
the Dutch cities, and much of it had to be built on piles. For his
Summer Palace he wanted a house which looked as though it
was made for work, and in this state, with contemporary furniture and some of Peter's instruments and maps, it is on view
today. He ordered something more elegant for his mistress
Catherine (a wooden structure which has disappeared), and something grander still after he had married her, and apparently he
had no objection to a comparatively grand house being erected, on
the Vasilievsky Ostrov embankment, for his favourite Menshikov,
the ex-stable boy and ex-pieman whom he made the first Governor
of St Petersburg. Severely simplified and somewhat spoiled in the
nineteenth century, this still stands as the Menshikov Museum,
bearing the date 1710. Later it was associated with a more dramatic date—17th June 1917, when it was the meeting-place of the
First All-Russian Congress of Soviets. The delegates were all a
good deal more revolutionary than Kerensky's Provisional
Government, but they were not sure what action they should
take, and the leader of their Menshevik group declared that there
was 'no political party at present able to take power and guarantee
leadership of the country'. To this Lenin called out from his seat
in words which have entered into Bolshevik legend: 'There is
such a Party!'

In 1710 Peter had the court and most of the administration
transferred from Moscow, and in 1712 he proclaimed his city the
capital of Russia. Here foreign ambassadors came to marvel at the

'barbarian' who had defeated Sweden and made Russia indubit-
ably a European power. Russia now built and sailed her men-of-
war on the Baltic—a provocation previously unheard of; she
had a great trading capital, visited by ships of all nations, and at
the extremities of her Empire she had added Kamchatka and the
Kurile Islands, while in the south she had taken Baku from the
Persians. Russia was Russia now, no longer Muscovy bumbling
away in the midst of an unknowable land, semi-Asiatic, semi-
Byzantine. The very name of Muscovy was reminiscent of the
days when it was no more than a Grand Duchy, whereas nowadays—to the scandal of the Austrian Emperor—Russia was declared an Empire. Peter had proclaimed himself Emperor, and
had had his second wife Catherine ('the German whore') crowned
as Empress, in the Cathedral of the Assumption in the Kremlin,
the traditional scene of Russian coronations.

At the new court in St Petersburg, or indeed anywhere else in
his dominions, Peter was shaving off the long, old Orthodox
beards of his boyars—shaving them with his own hands when he
felt like doing so; he was cutting off the long sleeves of their old
Russian gowns—again sometimes with his own hands; he was
forcing them into the West European dress of the period, such as
he wore himself; he was breaking up the quasi-Asiatic institution
of the *terem*, the harem-like seclusion in which Russian upper-
class women lived with their children, and he was dragging them,
tongue-tied and gauche in their European clothes, into his
assemblées where, by order, both sexes made conversation like
Western ladies and gentlemen, and they drank (in moderation)
and played cards, by order, while longing for the comfortable dis-
order, the drunkenness and familiar crudity of their life under the
old boyar regime. Nearly every detail of their sloppy old life had
a traditional religious sanction—even their sloppy old garments
and still more their shaggy hair: uncut beards, and uncut hair,
parted in the middle, were a sort of Nazirite indication of sanctity,
as they were—and usually still are even to this day—with

Orthodox priests. And worst, perhaps and most impious of all, this Tsar was smoking his long Dutch pipe like the Antichrist he surely was, and forcing the men in his *assemblées* to take pipes and blow their smoke over the women as well.

Besides all his successes in foreign, military and naval affairs, besides bringing the Church under State control (where it has remained ever since), besides founding a capital and dragging his nobles forcibly into the eighteenth century, Peter brought more innovations and stimulations into Russian life than one would expect from a whole committee of ardent reformers. To take only a few examples: he instituted the 'Table of Ranks', which imposed military or civilian service on all members of the nobility or squirearchy, but which also opened the services to the talents: anyone who could reach the fifth grade in the fourteen equivalent ranks of either service was automatically ennobled. He took a census (with a death penalty for avoidance), he preached that commerce and industry were occupations as honourable as public service, and he encouraged the iron industry of the Urals, partly by State enterprise. (In a few years Russia led the world in the production of iron.) He started up the first Russian newspaper, and the first public theatre, he got rid of some unnecessary letters from the Russian alphabet and he introduced a new typeface, on a Dutch model, which incidentally is much easier to read than the face now used every day in *Pravda*. He founded the Imperial Academy of Sciences, and he modernized the calendar. One New Year's Day Russians found they were instructed to set off rockets and light bonfires in order to greet, not the year 7208 since the creation of the world, as they expected, but under a new reckoning, the 1700th year since the birth of Christ.

The Westernization of Russia was not quite invented by Peter; it had had notable exponents in the previous century, but he hurried on the process enormously, against the general conservatism, and in an international situation which was now much more to Russia's advantage. Under the leadership of this extraordinary man the character of the Westernization, and particularly the character of the capital city, were affected fundamentally and in some ways indelibly. To understand the peculiar nature and significance of St Petersburg it is necessary to understand the character of its founder.

Peter's father died when he was three, and he was brought up in the *terem* by an adoring mother who was incapable of coping with such a high-spirited boy and gave him only a sycophant as a tutor. When he was ten he saw the bodies of courtiers, some of them his friends, hurled out of the windows of the Kremlin on to the pikes of the mutinous *streltsy*, the musketeer regiments, in the yard below. (He took an even bloodier revenge on the *streltsy* later.) He was soon beyond palace control and, to the general scandal, was educating himself among the foreigners of the 'German suburb'—in crafts, in foreign habits, in drinking, and in women. (The scandal was the foreigners rather than the women.) Deprived of a normal emotional development, his six-feet-seven of superhuman strength and inexhaustible energy were to go into organizing, ordering, drinking, leching, and above all into using his hands. He learned shipbuilding in Holland and at Deptford (where he was a pestilential guest to John Evelyn), he learned tooth-pulling, primitive surgery, bricklaying, the elements of engraving, printing, and metalworking; in the cathedral of St Peter and St Paul one can see the ivory candelabrum which he made with his own hands.

He had both boon companions and hardheaded counsellors, but in general he seems to have ranked human beings with the tools or objects which he knew so well how to use. Thousands admired and loved him and would follow him in any adventure, but he seemed shockingly short of understanding of other people's motives or of the concessions that might be made to them. He indulged in cruel horseplay and buffoonery—as others did in his age—but it seems less accurate to indict him for general cruelty than for an almost animal lack of sensibility. He had himself wheeled face foremost through Evelyn's favourite holly hedge and used Evelyn's pictures for pistol practice, as an unthinking lark. When he dealt with public affairs the sensibility was equally lacking, though he was serious, a good planner, and lucid in command; but he seemed to think that one simply made a decree and then people carried it out. Peter had little sense of history, and little sense of posterity. There is no room here to discuss why he rejected and eventually ordered the arrest and execution of his soft-natured son Alexis—whether it was unconscious revulsion from the idea that he must one day be succeeded or unconscious revenge for his own childhood, that motivated him to accept the allegations that Alexis, who asked for nothing but a quiet life, was the leader of the underground opposition to his reforms. (There certainly were those who would have liked to see Alexis fill this role.) Whatever Peter's reasons for ordering the execution the result was that he left no instructions for an heir. He had founded a city, St Petersburg was his greatest darling, his greatest created object, and it stood for the Russian State.

The 'window on Europe' theory of St Petersburg is inadequate if it implies that the city was founded simply for better communication with Europe, or to allow better imitation of Europe. St Petersburg was to be the assertion of the newly found, imperial, Russian power, and it was to be so far as practicable an assertion in European terms, yet by no means a mere pastiche of a European city. It was to be the assertion of Russia-in-Europe. The coronation of Tsars continued to take place in Moscow; right up to the last Romanov, no Tsar was ever crowned in St Petersburg. It is with St Petersburg, and Europeanization, that the tragic split began, however, between the culture and enlightenment of the privileged few and the grey level of the Russian mass, which was to be one of the ground causes in the end of Revolution. Today every visitor can see the equivocal character of the city reflected in its architecture and layout and the whole feel of the place. It is not quite Europe and not quite Russia—and all this goes back to Peter.

It is not surprising that Peter is respected and admired in Soviet times, both officially and privately, and even regarded with affection, in spite of his acts of tyranny and all the lives lost in the building of his city. He is admired for his modernization, for his founding of the city and for the recognition which he won for Russia as a great power. It is for this that the Bronze Horseman and other statues of Peter still stand in Leningrad, that his grave is the only Romanov grave which is today honoured with a wreath, that the Anthropological Museum still bears his name because he founded the collections, and that he is celebrated in art reproductions and even in a modern musical entitled *The Tobacco Captain*. (Russians do not now call him Peter the Great but Peter the First.) He left his mark in the very name of the city; true to his admiration for more advanced nations, he at first gave it a name he assumed to be Dutch—*Sankt Piterburkh*. But *Sankt* is not Dutch, but German, and Peter soon germanized the whole name into Sankt Peterburg, or Sankt Petersburg. To ordinary Russians this never evoked the idea of Saint Peter, because the Russian word for saint is *svyatoi*; *sankt* means nothing even to Church people, because their terminology comes from Greek, not Latin. The Orthodox Church never called it the city of 'Svyatoi' Peter; like everyone else they used 'Skt Peterburg' or 'Skt Petersburg' for addresses and so forth, but in ordinary contexts people simply called it 'Peterburg', pronounced in the German way but with the stress on the last syllable. It was the city of Peter rather than Saint Peter, and this was confirmed when at the outbreak of the First World War it was renamed Petrograd. But inhabitants and intimates of the city have always called it in conversation by the affectionately abbreviated name of 'Piter', from the original Dutch. Leningraders, speaking of home, still say 'Piter' today, and for all the city's association with Lenin, to call it 'Piter' is not felt to be anti-Soviet.

There are only a few buildings of Peter's time to be seen in Leningrad now, though the layout of the central parts of the city goes back to his period. The most striking façade is that of the Anthropological Museum on the bank of the Neva opposite the Admiralty, and next but one to it the university building, which is end on to the river. The museum, originally the home of the Academy of Sciences, was built by the German Mattarnovy and other German and Italian architects, the university by Trezzini and other Italians. It was erected to house, originally, the 'Twelve Colleges', the ministerial bodies set up by Peter, and its four-hundred-yard frontage, only three storeys high, still has the twelve porches and twelve dormers advanced at regular intervals. There is an old-fashioned neatness about both buildings which one might be tempted to call German, but the green-and-white stateliness of the buildings by the Neva seems to me more of an Italian than a northern severity. The museum is surmounted by a great tower with two lanterns, one above the other—a theme which has been copied again and again in Russian architecture.

The most charming survival is the Summer Palace, and behind it the Summer Garden, which was laid out by Leblond, a pupil of the great Le Nôtre, on the model of Versailles. Trees were brought from all over Russia, including some of the limes which still stand there, and fountains were engineered from the water of the canal which thus got its name of Fontanka. Classical statues were imported, many of which remain, and in the winter months they are encased in wooden boxes to protect them from the frost. Leblond became the Chief Architect of St Petersburg, and it was he who laid out the plan of the city, including the three grand avenues which radiate from the Admiralty Garden—the Nevsky, the Mayorova (formerly the Voznesensky), and the Ulitsa Dzerzhinskovo (formerly the Gorokhovaya) between them.

The Alexander Nevsky Monastery at the far end of the Nevsky Prospect remains a haven of peace. There are several eighteenth-century churches there now, but the large domed cathedral of the Annunciation, in a courtyard full of trees, is the one designed by Trezzini, and in its echoing interior one may like to recall that Peter, for all his iconoclasm, was a practising Orthodox, knew the liturgy by heart, and enjoyed sometimes singing in the choir. The greatest of Russian generals, Suvorov, was buried here in 1800.

But for the atmosphere of the early eighteenth century one must go to Hare Island, still enclosed in the fortress walls of St Peter and St Paul. Forgetting for a while what was suffered by so many in the notorious prison of the fortress, one should enter by one of the massive baroque gateways and linger in the cobbled squares and among the iron lamp-posts around the cathedral with its gleaming needle. The whole precinct is a neglected part of the city nowadays; the garrison does not seem an important one, there are waving willow trees and civilians fishing, weeds from the original delta flora are flowering in the cracks of the walls, and the only thing that seems to bring any number of Leningraders to Hare Island is the clean and sandy bathing beach in summer, where they can bask under the south rampart of their founder's fort.

Chapter 2

The Empresses

AFTER Peter's death Russia endured one of those periods, frequent in her history, when the succession was often in doubt. The throne was first occupied by Peter's widow, who reigned for two years as Catherine I, just long enough to humanize the lives of her subjects a little. She was succeeded by Peter II, son of the murdered Alexis, a promising boy of twelve who moved the capital back to Moscow but died before he was sixteen. The Empress Anna, who came next, moved it back to St Petersburg again, ordering all the merchants and artisans who had left it to return under penalty of forced labour. A coarse-natured and sometimes cruel woman, she did found a proper court, which was something Peter the Great had never been interested in. There were lavish banquets, balls and firework displays and the same kind of extravagance and show as in the other courts of Europe. When Peter had insisted on Western clothes he had been satisfied to see his boyars in the same sort of drab working suits that he wore himself, but now the court displayed expensive fabrics of every hue; no one of either sex was allowed to appear there twice in the same clothes. If we omit Ivan VI, who reigned only fourteen months as an infant, and Peter III, who was murdered after a few months on the throne, the rest of the century is spanned by the two great empresses who created so much of the baroque and classical glory of St Petersburg—Elizabeth (1741–61) and Catherine II (the Great) (1761–96).

The nobles had a great deal of their own way after Peter died; they got themselves out of service obligations by degrees and increased the burdens on the serfs, and some noble factions took

18

a hand in gerrymandering the succession. Some of them returned
thankfully to Moscow, which remained a centre for reactionaries
and those who considered themselves to be most truly Orthodox.
But even without the compulsions imposed by Anna, the attraction of Peter's city was too great. At his death the population was
about 40,000, by 1750 it had increased to 95,000, and when
Catherine took the throne in 1761 it had risen to 150,000, equal
to that of Moscow. Besides the court and the glamour of a
capital, what had the Petersburgers got?

They lived in a region so barren that, except for timber, water,
fish and a very little other food, all supplies had to come from great
distances. Their city was thus a magnet for domestic commerce,
and further, it was on its way to becoming Russia's greatest port.
It was the direct and easy channel for foreign goods, especially
luxuries. One of Anna's first acts was to abolish the import duties
on silk, woollen and cotton fabrics, wine, sugar, and dyes. In
return for these the Western countries were buying Russian
hemp, tallow, hides, canvas, flax, timber, linen, iron, and tar.
(Later in the century the British Admiralty became seriously
concerned at their almost total dependence on Russia for naval
supplies.) St Petersburg was a city for pioneers in trade or in
handicraft, and for unskilled labourers, a city where unencumbered
males could make their way; only 32 per cent of its population, at
the 1789 numbering, were women.

St Petersburg was a city which could spread freely to the
south, west, and east; there was no awkward historical legacy to
hold it up, only swamp-land and forest. The south of the city was
already laid out in a huge fan with three more or less concentric
canals cutting across the radiating avenues. No European capital
has had the same opportunity to grow to a preconceived design.
St Petersburg had no need for a ring of fortifications, since Sweden
had ceased to be any danger, and hence, unlike Moscow and
other old cities, she acquired no rings of extra-broad boulevards in
the place of fortifications which had been pulled down. However,

the nobility of the plan was by no means matched by the
houses. In the eighteenth century, and for most of the nineteenth,
the majority were still built of wood, as anywhere else in Russia,
and fires were frequent—as anywhere else in Russia. Only a few
main thoroughfares and squares were paved with cobbles, and
away from the centre all was mud in spring and autumn, or
whenever it chanced to rain, while even on the Nevsky the
swamp was still coming up through the paving-stones.

The climate of Leningrad is regarded by Russians as a trying
one, not because the city is so far north but because it is so much
under the influence of the sea and the westerly winds. It is an un-
certain climate, and most Russians are used to a dry, continental
type, with week after week of still, calm days in both winter and
summer. In Leningrad the thermometer falls to 18° Fah. in
winter, and often a good deal lower, the Neva is frozen over from
mid-November to early April on the average, and snow lies for at
least four and a half months in the year, but there may be a
maddening, unbearable thaw in January, perhaps, with bitter
damp winds from the Baltic. In summer the temperature may
rise as high as 91° Fah. but the season is as unpredictable as in
England; August is usually the wettest month, there can be fogs
or mists at almost any time, through the sudden changes of
temperature and humidity, and there is altogether too much rain
for Russian tastes. I had heard for years about the proverbial
rain in Leningrad, 'just like Manchester', but when I looked at the
official records I found that the annual rainfall is no more than
twenty-two inches—less than often falls on London. All this adds
up to what Russian works of reference call 'a mild climate', but
the Russians have no liking for such changeability and damp.
There are some beautiful pearly still days in summer, and pink
still days over the sparkling city in winter, but these are far outnumbered by grey days throughout the year. It is depressing when
the long winter nights give way, at about ten in the morning, to
heavy overcast skies, and even the famous 'white nights' of

Plan of St Petersburg in 1753 – Hare Island in the centre

The Hermitage and Winter Palace seen across the Neva

Palace Square with Rossi's General Staff Building and the Alexander Column (47·5 metres high), the tallest granite column in the world

The Old Admiralty, the central point of Leningrad's city plan

A White Night on the Griboyedov
Canal, with the Church of the
Saviour 'on the Blood'

Spring on the Neva, opposite the fortress and
Cathedral of St Peter and St Paul

One of the rostral columns commemorating naval
victories; the view is from the steps of the Bourse
across the Neva to the bathing beach and Cathedral
of St Peter and St Paul

Smolny, the Leningrad
headquarters of the
Communist Party,
formerly a boarding-
school for daughters of
the nobility and gentry

The 'Kunstkamer' or
Anthropological
Museum, founded by
Peter the Great, seen
across the Neva

June are by no means all as magical as they are in literature; a white night streaming with rain is more insistent and miserable than a streaming dark night.

The climate is like the city, not quite Russian and not quite 'European'. It seems significant that the horse chestnut, which Westerners expect to see in the avenues of any nobly planted city, can only survive in Russia proper on the extreme western fringes of the country. Scuffling one's feet through the crisp dry leaves at Peterhof in September, one could imagine one was about to enter the park at Versailles. But Moscow has nothing comparable.

There could have been no more brilliant Empress than Elizabeth to set St Petersburg ablaze against its grey skies. She was known as the best dancer and one of the most beautiful women in Europe. She was goodhearted on the whole, plump (because she could never resist good food) and as the English Ambassador delicately put it, 'she hadn't an ounce of nun's flesh about her'. Her lovers were few in number, however, far less notorious than those of her successor Catherine, and when they were cast off they were not dismissed from her friendship. She was even more prodigal than Anna in balls and fêtes and masquerades, and there were 15,000 dresses in her wardrobes when she died. Very often she announced that the court would hold a 'metamorphosis'— a ball where the women were obliged to wear men's clothes and the men had to dress in hoop skirts and panniers. There was, however, nothing more perverse in this than Elizabeth's desire to show off her very presentable legs and feet; she often appeared dressed as a Dutch sailor, in compliment to her father Peter the Great. Her tables were loaded with foreign delicacies, including the first pineapples ever to reach Russia, and drunkenness at court was not merely no longer normal—it was outlawed on all but exceptional occasions.

Elizabeth's rule coincided most fortunately with the working life of the brilliant and prolific architect Rastrelli. The son of a

c

Florentine sculptor whom Peter had brought to St Petersburg,
he was considerably Russianized, he studied the peculiarities of
Russian church architecture, and he absorbed them into the
unique, grandiloquent, often over-ornamented style of his master-
pieces—the Winter Palace, the Great Palace at Tsarskoe Selo,
the Smolny monastery and church, a great part of Peterhof, and
private palaces in Petersburg such as the Stroganov Palace, where
the Nevsky Prospect crosses the Moika Canal. His version of the
baroque, it has been pointed out, recalls the Zwinger in Dresden
or the Viennese palaces built by Fischer von Erlach, rather than
the Italian style. But none of these show the riotous colours
typical of Rastrelli. He was short of natural building stone and
so, perhaps in consequence, he created the great stucco façades and
painted them in colours which one would not imagine stucco
could bear if one was familiar only with Italian work. Deep azure
blue, pistachio green, olive green, chocolate, and purple, as well
as the familiar terracottas and Venetian reds, pink, ochres and
lemon yellows, all picked out in white or black—these were the
colours to affront the gloomy northern skies, and they became
established as the colours for classical façades all over Russia.
The paint is constantly renewed on them today, and the colours
are still sometimes used on a new building when a small stucco or
wooden erection is needed. But the dripping swages and garlands,
the bewigged window-heads on the Winter Palace, the overmuscled
titans rising out of stucco swaddlings on the façade at Tsarskoe
Selo, the rows of statues on skylines (and originally they were
gilded statues)—such extravagances remained the mark of Rastrelli's exuberant manner alone; they had few successors.

Rastrelli's Winter Palace, with its long, operatic frontage on
the Neva embankment, is the fifth palace of that name. It was not
particularly a palace for winter use: when Peter had the original
little building put up in 1711 it was simply called after the 'Winter
Ditch' (*zimnyaya kanavka*) on whose brink it stood. Peterhof also
had earlier origins: the main block is more or less by Leblond,

and scattered about the gardens are some little pavilions unaltered since Peter's day. But the ornate, imperial appearance of the palace, and much of the interior, and above all the two daring low wings, each crowned with a superb, topheavy—imperial orb?—turban?—derivative of an onion dome?—all that is Rastrelli's.

Peterhof stands on a natural escarpment, looking down a long, narrow ornamental water, lined with spouting fountains, to the Gulf of Finland. It was intended to be the Russian Versailles, though it was superseded later by Tsarskoe Selo. Nowadays all the country palaces have become places to visit at week-ends, but Peterhof, with its splendid site, is the most popular. One can go by train or bus, eat at the open-air restaurant discreetly hidden in the gardens, and return to Leningrad by boat. Leblond and Rastrelli excelled themselves in the terrace of gushing fountains and gilded statues which plunges down from the great promenade in front of the palace, where you look down on the canal to the sea; and though Western visitors sometimes find this cascade too flamboyant to bear close inspection, Russians seem to admire the rococo elements as well as the magnificent ensemble. They find further reason for pride and admiration in the work of restoration. During the war Peterhof was all but wrecked, but recently one has been able to see it recover year by year, as the fabric was first made firm and restored in every detail of its almond green and white, and then the work began on the interior, where the hangings, the gildings, the wallpapers, and even the 328 portraits of the prettiest women of Elizabeth's court, by the undistinguished artist Rotari, are being re-created where they cannot be restored. No wonder they make visitors put on canvas overshoes to shuffle over the polished floors under the jealous eye of the old women in head-scarves. Peterhof is one of the symbols of victory; one must call it now by its Russianized name of Petrodvorets.

Tsarskoe Selo ('The Tsar's Village') is supposed to be called Pushkin, but it had already been renamed once since the Revolution as Detskoe Selo ('Children's Village'), because of its many

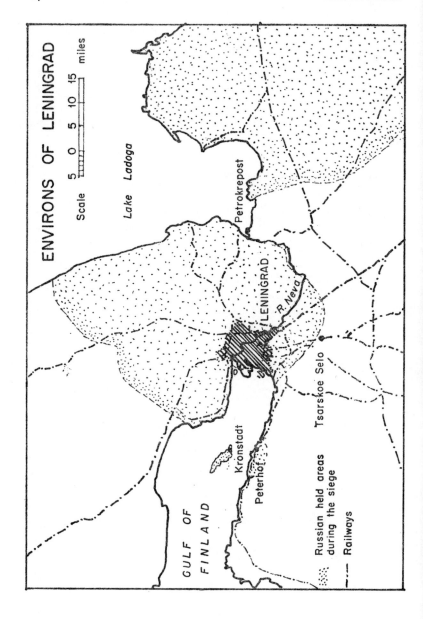

ENVIRONS OF LENINGRAD

Scale

5   0   5   10   15   miles

Lake Ladoga

Petrokrepost

LENINGRAD

R. Neva

Tsarskoe Selo

Kronstadt

Peterhof

GULF OF FINLAND

Russian held areas
during the siege

Railways

holiday homes for children. The association with Pushkin is less than his association with several places in Leningrad. At eighteen miles or so west of Leningrad the countryside is quite hilly, and the palaces of Tsarskoe Selo are also planted on little elevations, though not so dramatically as Peterhof. Besides sightseeing, one of the week-end attractions here is rowing on the lake, where Rastrelli's little 'Grotto' pavilion still stands at the water's edge.

Palaces and an extravagant court were by no means the only results of Elizabeth's reign. She chose her advisers well and was fortunate in her generals. During the Seven Years War her troops occupied Berlin, struck terror into the Prussians under Frederick the Great at the battle of Kunersdorf, and became recognized by all Europe as formidable fighters. Peter had forced Europe to take notice of Russia; under Elizabeth Russia won a firm place among European nations.

Catherine was German by birth and education, and came to the throne only through her marriage to the hopeless Peter III, who idolized Frederick the Great. There was a great turn of policy, and peace between Russia and Prussia, or Germany, until 1914. Catherine's armies turned against the hereditary enemy Turkey, and against Poland. Huge tracts of land were added through the three partitions of Poland, and in the south the whole of the steppe, the Crimea, and the Sea of Azov were cleared at last. From this time began the fears of a Russian threat to the overland route to India, and the Anglo-French propping up of Turkey which led, among other things, to the Crimean War. The southern conquests cleared an enormous area for the growing of grain, and this made an important counterbalance to the regions of serfdom, for most of the inhabitants of this 'New Russia' settled, inevitably, as free men. There was grain for export before long, some through the new port of Odessa, but much of the new wealth flowed back to St Petersburg, and for this and other reasons the merchant population of the capital doubled its numbers in forty years.

However, merchants were 'recommended to be modest in their houses and their equipages', since they were not nobles. They had to wait another century before they could rise in society, but meanwhile their money power continually increased.

There was no bourgeois vulgarity about the growth of Petersburg under Catherine—very much the opposite. Even before the end of Elizabeth's reign the baroque style was felt to be over-assertive, and Catherine replaced Rastrelli by other architects. The Academy of Fine Arts had been founded in 1757 with the French architect Vallin De La Motte as its President, and largely under his influence a more severe French style replaced the baroque, to be reinforced later in Catherine's reign by the remarkable work and influence of the Scotsman Charles Cameron, by the work of the Italians Quarenghi and Rinaldi, and by many native architects working in the same tradition.

Catherine was impassioned for building, as for all the arts, and she encouraged them with immense prodigality. (She bought just about half of all the best pictures in the Hermitage.) She was not, however, spending simply for herself; she was nothing like so feminine as Elizabeth, and her court was rather prim, more noted for philosophers than for fêtes. It is hardly unkind to say that the catalogue of her amours suggests a Teutonic passion for organization as well as her declared passion for the bed. (Incidentally she was by no means as good-looking as the actresses who have portrayed her in films.) She had read widely and deeply during the boring years of her marriage, she had prepared herself to be Empress, and as a German she knew that it was all the more important for her to glorify the Russian State. Her ceaseless range of activities was almost as vast as that of Peter the Great. She never let private affairs interfere with public; the ugly, one-eyed Potemkin was assigned great duties, including the government of the whole of 'New Russia', because of his outstanding ability as a general and an administrator, but usually her lovers received no such promotion. She was not successful in internal reform;

she was too theoretical, and Russia's appalling domestic problems were perhaps already beyond solution by even a politically-minded autocrat. She was not really an intellectual, though she corresponded regularly with Voltaire, Diderot and D'Alembert and liked to think herself a member of the European intellectual *élite*. But she did found educational establishments of all grades, she encouraged men of all kinds of ability, including the polymath Lomonosov, whose great contribution as a writer was to establish a coherent Russian literary language. She established French as the language of the court, the nobility, and the educated, which brought those classes well into the European stream, and this set up the tradition of speaking French in preference to Russian or even to the exclusion of Russian, which lasted until the Revolution. (One can still meet, in Leningrad or Moscow, courteous elderly academics or theatre people who learned their excellent French from governesses in the old way before 1917.)

In opening up Russia to the language and thought of France, Catherine inevitably let in the first wave of liberal ideas—from Voltaire, from her favourite Montesquieu and the other Encyclopédistes, and eventually from the French Revolution itself, which had many admirers in Petersburg. At this Catherine took fright, banned the *Encyclopédie*, broke off relations with France, and clamped down heavily on liberal ideas. Alexander Radishchev, the author of the first reformist work in Russian, *A Journey from St Petersburg to Moscow* (1790), received a death sentence from Catherine, later commuted to exile, for his revelation of the misery, poverty, corruption and hopelessness which he found on his 'Journey'. 'My soul was afflicted by the sufferings of humanity', wrote Radishchev in his book, thereby establishing, it was later to be said, the birth of the Russian intelligentsia. For this Russian word, in the sense in which Russians used it all through the next century, meant not simply intellectuals but the educated class *who were concerned for their tragic country and who strove to take action*. Early in her reign Catherine had played with the

condemnation of serfdom as an evil (almost a century before it
was eventually abolished), but when autocracy, the vehicle of all
her energies, was threatened, she took fright. In fact she founded a
special department, the forerunner of the Okhrana and the Soviet
Cheka, 'to punish anyone infected, or suspected of being infected, with the pernicious poison of liberal thought'.

The legacy of her reign in more enlightened ways, however, was
very considerable. She imported foreign ballet masters and danc-
ers and lavished money on performances. (The very first ballets
in Russia had been presented in 1727, under Catherine I.) Newspapers and periodicals flourished, including some satirical jour-
nals on the foreign model, which sometimes held up class privi-
lege to ridicule. Hospitals were founded, including the first
maternity hospital. Science, already set well on its way by Peter,
was now flourishing. Lomonosov, among his multifarious activities, described the nature of the atmosphere on Venus, and ob-
served the transit of that planet through a telescope made by the
English instrument-maker James Short. The School of Mines,
the oldest higher technical institution in Russia, was founded in
1773.

Trade and industry of course increased enormously; one of
Catherine's first acts was to abolish the old monopolies. From this
period dates the measure of the 'St Petersburg standard' for
timber (165 cubic feet or 1980 board feet), which is still used
for British timber imports, though usually without the 'St Petersburg' prefix. Besides iron and metalworking and shipbuilding
industries, the capital was now producing much of its own sugar,
paper, tobacco, and textiles. Most luxury goods still came from
abroad, but the output of the Imperial Porcelain Factory, re-
fined by a chemist who worked with Lomonosov, itself now
entered the luxury class, rivalling the products of Meissen, and
it has kept that standard ever since. Founded in 1744, the factory
is now called after Lomonosov himself.

The architecture of Catherine's time still forms a great part of

what gives most pleasure in the city and its environs. De La
Motte, with Kokorinov, built the Academy of Fine Arts which
stands on the same river frontage as the Anthropological Museum; it looks even more European, rather Louis Quinze. He also
built the huge general store, the Gostinny Dvor, on the Nevsky,
which is one of the buildings seen by foreigners on even the
shortest visit. A two-storeyed, many-arched edifice, covering
a great area but consisting largely of a number of small compart-
ments, it seems maddeningly ill-adapted to the crowds of contemporary shoppers. It was not built as a general store, however, but
in order to house scores of little shops under one roof, where
they could have common protection from the cold and from theft.
The façade on the Nevsky Prospect was altered, not for the
better, in the late nineteenth century. De La Motte's best work
is the 'Small' Hermitage, the original Hermitage in fact, which
now forms part of the continuous great frontage—Winter Palace
(1754–62)—Small Hermitage (1764–7)—Old Hermitage (1771–
84)—Hermitage Theatre (1783–7, by Quarenghi)—New Hermitage (1839–52). In spite of varying dates and architects they make
a harmonious ensemble, and the whole constitutes the colossal
Hermitage Museum of today. The term 'Hermitage' may suggest
the artificiality of Marie Antoinette, but De La Motte's building is
really small and intimate; it was built at Catherine's order as a
refuge from the grandeur of the Winter Palace, so that she could
meet men of learning and artists, as she loved to do, in surroundings created for the purpose. Between the Old Hermitage and the
Hermitage Theatre is the Winter Ditch, now one of the quietest
and most romantic little canals in Leningrad, spanned by the
first-floor gallery joining the two buildings.

Quarenghi built the Academy of Sciences, next to the university,
the riding school of the horse guards, the Yusupov Palace (where
Rasputin was murdered), the hospital on Liteiny Prospect (now
the Kuibyshev Hospital), the Alexander Palace and several smaller
buildings at Tsarskoe Selo, and above all the beautifully pro-

portioned Smolny Institute, once a severe boarding-school for noblemen's daughter's, then Lenin's headquarters, and still the headquarters of the Communist Party in Leningrad. All these are in a Palladian style of great dignity and simplicity. Quarenghi's work, however, is usually felt to be a little severe in comparison with the works of Cameron, such as the noble classical wing, the 'Cameron Gallery', which he added at Tsarskoe Selo. Cameron's masterpiece is the imperial palace at Pavlovsk, with its beautifully displayed crescent façade. Tamara Talbot Rice says in her *Concise History of Russian Art*:* 'Pavlovsk has been compared to Adam's Kedleston, but although Cameron must have greatly admired the Adam brothers, since he worked in the style they had made fashionable in England, his buildings are even more elegant and imaginative, and blend more naturally and harmoniously with their settings. He comes closer to Vanbrugh in his power of associating a building with its surroundings than does any other British architect.'

Painted stucco had given way to clean stone and often to expensive natural materials, superlatively so in the Marble Palace built by Rinaldi (now the Lenin Museum). Finally one should quote the Tavrida or Taurida Palace, built by Starov and Volkov as a mansion for Potemkin, later the seat of the Duma, and after the Revolution the scene of many memorable assemblies. It is as cool and clean a building, all in white, as anything in Washington D.C. In fact all the buildings quoted are very close parallels to the great buildings in Britain of the same period—say, Chiswick House, Mereworth, or Osterley. They are similar in style, and in the strewing of obelisks and miniature Greek temples through the grounds, but they are not similar in social weight and significance, because in the eighteenth century our social structure was already different. For the equivalent of the middle-class delights of the British period—say, the Bath terraces or the older parts of Bloomsbury—there is practically nothing to show in Leningrad,

* Thames and Hudson, 1963.

and this was extremely characteristic both of old St Petersburg and of Russia in general. Still less is there any trace of the huts, shacks, or hovels in which the workers who built all these palaces spent their lives. Those who built the Winter Palace lived in dugouts in what is now the Palace Square throughout the year. Those who lined the Neva and the great canals with pink granite —another work of Catherine's reign—had to continue through all weathers and all seasons, and in 1787 they marched, one man chosen from every ten, to the Winter Palace to protest. This was not the first protest by the workers of St Petersburg; there was a big one in 1774. Their protests were recorded by the police who arrested them or chased them away with blows, and the records have been preserved, but of their homes, of any equivalent to the humblest English cottage, there is no vestige.

Catherine bequeathed a greater class division to St Petersburg and to Russia than she found when she came to the throne. But she bequeathed also the grand manner, to be developed still further, and beautifully, by her immediate successors; she bequeathed the feeling for the grand statement, the polished marble or granite insistence which the Soviet regime has taken over in, for example, the stations of the Moscow or Leningrad Metro, the Lenin tomb, or the new provincial opera houses. To a Party which was consciously leading a nation of the oppressed, the dwellings of whose ancestors had left no trace, such assertion in the years of victory comes naturally enough.

Chapter 3

Repression, Reform, and Revolution

BACKWARD as Russia was, lagging by centuries behind Western Europe in some ways, she suffered the same new strains as Western countries in the nineteenth century, in addition to her ancient burdens. In Russia as elsewhere it was above all the century of industrialization, and because of industrialization it was the century also of mounting pressure for political reform. But large-scale industrialization came late to Russia, and except during the reign of Alexander II (1855–81), the Liberator who freed the serfs, and for a short time under Alexander I, there was unrelenting repression of free opinion, and resistance by the autocracy to the establishment of any form of national representative government. St Petersburg became a great industrial city, and by the end of the century it was turning out one-eighth of the country's output, but it was a city of growing misery, of arrests and assassinations, the headquarters of the 'Third Section', the secret police.

For Russia the nineteenth century was also the century of that astonishing cultural flowering which began with Pushkin and Krylov, Griboyedov and Gogol in literature, and Glinka, Dargomizhsky and others in music. It was also the century of great scientists, beginning with Mendeleyev (1834–1907), whose Periodic Table of Elements is the foundation of modern chemistry, and who predicted the existence of germanium, which we use in our radios, before it had been discovered in nature. At the same time Dokuchayev (1846–1903), 'the father of soil science', was at work; he was the first to study soil as a natural substance and not simply as a mineral, but his ideas were not known outside Russia until after his death. There was Pavlov (1849–1936) conducting his experiments on dogs and on the human nervous system, and there was Yablochkov (1847–94), who invented the electric bulb before Edison, used it to light a St Petersburg theatre in 1879, and sold some of his bulbs to Glasgow, where they were known as 'Yablochkov's candles'. All these men lived in St Petersburg, and some of their houses are turned into museums of their work today. Science helped educated Russians to appreciate the huge potentialities of their country, and made the police state look the more ridiculous by contrast. Science and industry together made the position of the autocracy and the significance of St Petersburg itself, perched at the Baltic corner of the country, more and more anomalous.

As to the writers, they were without exception opposed to the autocracy and on the side of reform; almost every Russian writer of note was at some time imprisoned for his opinions, exiled, or at least put under police supervision. There was never a Russian Macaulay or Kipling to sing the praises of native institutions; they sang the praises of the Russian people, of 'our poor Russia' with her potentialities unrealized. This is true even of the first (and greatest), Pushkin (1799–1837). Dostoevsky pointed out in his memorial speech delivered in 1880:

'Pushkin with his profound insight . . . was the first to detect and expose the principal symptom of the sickness of our intellectual society, uprooted as it is from the soil and raised above the people. He set before us in relief our negative type, the disturbed and unsatisfied man.' And he quotes Pushkin's Aleko, who tried to find escape among the gypsies, and the Byronic figure of Eugene Onegin, as the forerunners of a host of others: Pechorin in Lermontov's *A Hero of Our Time*, Chichikov in Gogol's *Dead Souls* (i.e. 'Dead Serfs'), Rudin, the hero of Turgenev's novel of that name, and Bolkonsky in *War and Peace*.

However, most of the writers, composers, and other creative artists continued to live, when they were allowed to, in St Petersburg, where they formed circles of their own, and for those who could afford it the city continued to be a modish centre of striking brilliance and beauty, fit to compare with any capital in Europe. The first half of the century saw the completion, on the grandest scale, of the city's great classical heritage of architecture. Rossi (a Russian in spite of his name) was the greatest master of townscape. At the back of the Winter Palace he built the War Office in quite a different style, but he integrated the architecture of the Palace Square superbly by joining both buildings in the huge archway which leads out to the Nevsky, and by diverting attention towards the slender, very tall pink column in the centre of the square, a memorial to Alexander I. The Palace Square was later the scene of workers' demonstrations, and today it remains empty, little used by traffic, except when crowds gather for 7th November or 1st May; on ordinary days it is a breathtaking open space. When Rossi built the Alexandrinsky Theatre (now the Pushkin Theatre) he was able also to design the short street leading to it (now called Rossi Street), each side being a single block. The beautifully colonnaded façade of the Russian Museum of Art (originally the Mikhailov Palace), and the square of which it forms one side, are also Rossi's; the neighbouring streets also formed part of an ensemble designed by him, but they were largely rebuilt, and the prospects spoiled, at the end of the century. After the last war, however, a good deal was restored to his original design. Rossi's work is more magnificent than anything built by Nash in London, but it is pre-eminently a city architecture.

The best-known building in Leningrad is still the Admiralty, by Zakharov, which stands at the river end of the Nevsky Prospect. Its slender gilt spire, and the four-sided colonnade supporting it, rest on an immensely heavy pavilion with a small entrance arch beneath, reminiscent of the massive old Russian gates at Vladimir or Novgorod, and this great block is used to break up the quarter-mile of Regency-type frontage.

There were two attempts to give St Petersburg a cathedral to rival St Peter's in Rome—the Kazan Cathedral and St Isaac's, both of which, like Peter the Great's cathedral, are clean outside the Orthodox tradition of church architecture. The Kazan Cathedral, by Voronikhin, the serf who became a great architect, has an Italianate dome and a great semi-circular colonnade sweeping out in two arms in front, on the Nevsky. St Isaac's is more in the style of a gigantic St Paul's, but is built of polished granite and other more valuable stones. It has room for 13,000 people, and its great golden cupola is visible from all over the city and to this day is the favourite vantage-point for looking over Leningrad. Its architect was the Frenchman Montferrand, who ran into such difficulties that a committee of Russian architects had to be appointed to help him finish the job, which took forty years.

The famous Bourse (now the Naval Museum), in the great sweep of the Neva by the promontory of the Vasilievsky Ostrov, was designed by the Swiss Thomas de Thomon, on the model of the Temple of Poseidon at Paestum. A rust-red and white building, it concentrates the eye on its salient position, all the better for being low. In front of it, at the water's edge, rise the two pink granite columns by the same architect, a hundred feet high but immensely stout; they bear carved rostra, the beaks of ships, in Roman fashion, as a tribute to Russian naval victories. This is the most splendid point from which to take in the wide expanse of the Neva, here almost like an inland sea, with the Winter Palace on the embankment to one's right, and round to the left, further off one sees the Peter–Paul fortress and cathedral lying, as it were, low in the water. Here by the Bourse the river is so wide that there was only a bridge of boats, until 1850, to join the northern and southern halves of the city. Today there is more than one bridge over the Neva, but their bascules are raised and left open all night for ships to pass, so that after a late party one can be marooned on one side of Leningrad until the engineer comes to close the bridges again at four or five in the morning.

Until recent times there were fairs on this great stretch of the Neva when it froze in winter, with sledges drawn by reindeer, ice sports, ice palaces, and even first-class horse-races, but the chance of a sudden thaw is today regarded as too dangerous; about all that happens now is a little fishing through holes in the ice.

The Neva is deep, clean water emptying out of the biggest lake in Europe, Lake Ladoga, forty-six miles away. St Petersburg always drank Neva water, and Leningrad drinks it too; and though something like twenty thousand corpses from the last war lie deep in Ladoga, Leningrad is still able to purify the Neva, today using, I am told, an ultra-violet process. In 1837 the German J. G. Kohl,* one of the first compilers of travel books, described the anxiously awaited moment of the breaking up of the ice in spring, with everyone laying bets on the day it would happen:

No sooner have the dirty masses of ice advanced sufficiently to display as much of the bright mirror of the river as may suffice to bear a boat from one side to the other, than the glad tidings are announced to the inhabitants by the artillery of the fortress. At that moment, be it day or night, the commandant, arrayed in all the insignia of his rank, and accompanied by his officers, embarks in an elegant gondola and repairs to the emperor's palace which lies opposite. He fills a large crystal goblet with the water of the Neva, and presents it to the emperor, who drinks it off to the health of his dear citizens. There is not probably another glass of water that brings a better price, for it is customary for the emperor to fill the goblet with ducats before he returns it to the commandant. Such at least was the custom, but the goblet was found to have a sad tendency to enlarge its dimensions, so that the emperor began to perceive that he had every year a larger dose of water to drink, and a greater amount of ducats to pay for it. At last he thought it high time to compromise matters with his commandant, who now receives on each occasion a fixed sum of 200 ducats.

Some such ceremony might well be revived; the break-up of the

* *Russia*, English edition 1842.

ice is as dramatic as ever, and the sudden coming of the northern spring some time in April as eagerly awaited. 'The violent Russian spring', says Stravinsky (another St Petersburger), 'that seemed to begin in an hour and was like the whole earth cracking. That was the most wonderful event of every year of my childhood.'

But if the old merrymaking and ceremonial have gone, the buildings remain. The first half of the nineteenth century set the seal on the classical appearance of St Petersburg and established its porticoes and pediments as the only honourable style for mansions all over Russia. Even today in the provinces new buildings are sometimes erected in the same style, with hollow columns, maybe, of mere plywood. The Admiralty spire, too, is repeated in a thousand tawdry wooden pavilions at landing stages all over the country. And the low-hipped, almost flat roofs of Russian cities date from this period; they are made of sheet iron, and the idea is not to shed the snow, for that would impede the traffic, but to bear it comfortably until the spring, when the doormen, or *dvorniks,* get up on the roofs and shovel it all down in one great mess. These flattish roofs are usually red, with paint or with rust, so that the summer effect of the housetops in Leningrad is more like that of an Italian than a northern city.

All these urban patterns established themselves during the reigns of Paul I (1796–1801) and Alexander I (1801–25), and the earlier years of Alexander's brother Nicholas I, the 'policeman-Tsar'. With his reign the good architecture ended; he supported the ballet lavishly, and opened the collection of pictures in the Hermitage to the public for the first time, but he had little taste in architecture, and from 1843 allowed property owners to build as they wished, so long as their houses remained at least six feet less in height than the imperial palace. The rest of the Tsarist period saw the same uncontrolled exploitation of sites for industrial purposes, the same unhappy mixture of styles or absence of style in commercial buildings, and the same tasteless or florid

D

houses for business men, as in other European cities. Some startling Art Nouveau buildings were erected for *nouveaux riches* at the
end of the century, but few of these were in St Petersburg. And
there was some revival of old Slavonic styles, parallel to the
English Gothic revival, which produced churches such as the
knobbly red and gold Church of the Saviour 'On the Blood',
just off the Nevsky by the Griboyedov Canal. Meant as a copy of
St Basil's Cathedral in Moscow, it is clumsy and lifeless, and bears
the same relationship to St Basil's that some English suburban
churches do to the medieval cathedrals on which they are modelled.
The Church 'On the Blood' was erected to mark the spot where
Alexander II was assassinated, but this was a bad position for a
church, and it bears no decent relation to the surrounding buildings. Good neighbourliness in building and townscape was becoming forgotten. Early in the twentieth century the *Mir Iskusstva*
group and the 'Friends of St Petersburg' founded a society to
defend the beauties of the city, but they had little success.

The new industrial wealth helped of course to stimulate the
arts and sciences: it provided the magazines and publishing
houses which printed (when they were not censored) the works of
Dostoevsky, Turgenev, or Tolstoy, and it contributed lavish support for the operas of Tchaikovsky, Moussorgsky, and Borodin,
the ballets of Petipa, Benois, Fokine, and Bakst, or the theatrical
innovations of Meyerhold. But on the other hand, besides en-
gendering misery for millions, industrial wealth was unable to do
anything to solve the problems of a governmental system which
became more and more of an anachronism.

The assassination of the 'mad Tsar', Paul I, in 1801, marked the
end of an epoch. The unfortunate Paul was hopelessly unstable—
probably owing to the miserable neglect with which his mother,
Catherine the Great, treated him in childhood—and one result of
his paranoia was that he cut down the privileges of the nobles.
A group of them, therefore, with the connivance of his son
Alexander, murdered him in the building which is now the

Russian Museum of Art. Alexander I became the romantic hero-emperor who defeated Napoleon, rode into Paris at the head of his army, and impressed the whole of Europe. But at home he failed to make good the promise of some early liberal attitudes, and if he had not died unexpectedly he would probably have been assassinated too. He, however, was the target of no palace cabal, but of the first truly political conspirators in Russian history, the 'Decembrists'.

Members of the upper class, the corps of officers, and intellectuals, and eventually members of all classes, were becoming conscious of the backward state of the whole country, and they were no longer conspiring against a particular Tsar but against the whole regime. The Decembrists were mainly officers of noble birth who had been with Alexander to Europe and had seen the state of other nations at first hand. Their programme included the abolition of serfdom, a constitutional monarchy (or a republic), trial by jury, and civil liberties. In December 1825, baulked in their plan to assassinate Alexander, they organized a military rebellion against his successor, on the Senate Square in St Petersburg. They were amateurish and poorly led, and Nicholas I broke them up. Five were executed and more than a hundred punished, but the whole affair was supposed to be hushed up as too 'dangerous' to mention. The memory of this first revolt, however, inspired revolutionaries all through the century, and the Soviet Government has renamed the Senate Square, where the Bronze Horseman stands, as the Square of the Decembrists.

Nicholas I was already a martinet by temperament and training, and the Decembrist plot confirmed him implacably in the organizing of a police State in Russia. The Third Department supervised the whole population, largely by a network of informers, censorship was made severe to the point of idiocy, foreign travel was again prohibited as it had been under Paul, and every kind of intellectual activity was under suspicion. In the eighteenforties a civil servant, Petrashevsky, organized a discussion circle

attended by people of middle rank, including the young Dostoevsky. They discussed socialist theorists such as Louis Blanc, and
agreed that military rebellion could achieve nothing by itself; a
revolution must be supported by the masses. The police got to
hear of the group, as usual, and as usual succeeded in introducing
an informer. In 1849 the members were arrested, and twenty-one
young men, including Dostoevsky, were sentenced to death 'to
teach them a lesson'. Dostoevsky's description of the grim ceremony on the parade ground is known to everyone; it was Nicholas himself who decided the details—the white shirts, the sword
broken over their heads, the last prayers, and the drum roll which
was to continue until the messenger galloped up with the reprieve,
commuting the sentences to imprisonment in Siberia. Nicholas
liked well-drilled ceremonies, the same as he liked a well-drilled
ballet.

To Herr Kohl in 1837 things appeared superficially to be well
run, at least in St Petersburg. He even admired the Aliens' Office:
'Every thing issuing from these officials has the smoothest ex-
terior. Paper, writing, sealing, typographical arrangement, and
even the style of the passports, permissions to reside, certificates,
and testimonials which the Russians issue are better and more
tasteful in appearance than with us. Ours still bear the stamp of
the Middle Ages; in Russia all these things are in the newest
fashion.' St Petersburg and the whole of Russia were weighed
down by bureaucracy, accompanied inevitably by corruption as
the necessary lubricant. This is a condition which Russia has never
been able to shake off, and today the characters of the nineteenth-
century satirists—Gogol's Inspector-General, the smart swindler
Chichikov in *Dead Souls*, the bumbling provincials in the sketches
of Saltykov-Shchedrin, or the bitingly described officials in the
stories of Leskov—all these are so familiar to Soviet Russians
that their names are regularly used to characterize the modern
bureaucrats, sharks, and speculators, and especially the bureaucrats, who are so frequently exposed in the Soviet Press.

All these satirical writers worked in St Petersburg, and their honoured graves, along with those of Turgenev, Goncharov (the author of *Oblomov*), Belinsky, and a dozen more of Russia's greatest writers are ranged today in 'Authors' Avenue' in the Volkov Cemetery.

There were so many brilliant writers at work during the reign of Nicholas I that a great deal got published in spite of the censorship, although some of the most gifted, such as Herzen, had to take refuge abroad. But satire was one thing: constructive political work was quite another. There was no representative government, and it was all but impossible to get practical experience of the work of government. This was a handicap which reduced reformers for eighty years to either impotent discussion and theorizing or the sterile plotting of assassinations. Dostoevsky's novel *The Devils* (or *The Possessed*) gives a perfect picture of a revolutionary circle in mid century. They could not, for some decades to come, learn even how to revolt successfully, but meanwhile Tsars, their ministers, and their police chiefs had to fear the hand of the assassin, male or female, in the street, at the corner of a St Petersburg canal, on a train journey, and wherever they went.

When Nicholas died in 1855 most of Europe, as well as nearly all his subjects, rejoiced. It was ironical that he died in his bed, while his son Alexander II, the most enlightened Tsar ever to sit on the throne, was assassinated in 1881 just as he was about to grant the country a constitution. Alexander not only freed the serfs, he set up an independent judiciary for the first time in Russia, he started some primary education in the cities, and he established an elected council, the *zemstvo*, in every country district, and municipal councils in the towns. But though he removed many of his father's prohibitions and relaxed the censorship (so that the press was freer than it is in Soviet Russia today), there was still no administration but the old police administration. As so often happens when the regime of a tyrant comes to an end,

his successor, whatever liberties he may accord, is attacked by
some factions for not according more. So it was with Alexander.
He was loved and admired by his people, but hated, as a symbol
rather than as a person, by the revolutionaries. When repression
clamped down again under his son, the bearlike Alexander III,
and his grandson, the ungifted Nicholas II, the revolutionaries
realized that assassination, even of a Tsar, seemed to achieve
nothing. The more hardheaded of them began to study the whole
structure and facts of Russia's situation, which the best of them,
and particularly the Social Democrats, came to understand much
better than their rulers did. The death of Alexander thus removed
the chance of a constitution which might—and one must emphasize 'might'—have forestalled revolution, but it gave an
incentive for some of the country's best brains to study how a
revolution might be made effective.

After the Emancipation of 1861 both rulers and revolutionaries
had an entirely new situation to face. The Emancipation freed
forty million peasants, but most of them considered they had
been cheated, because they still had not been given their land:
they had to pay redemption annuities for twenty years to their
former landlords. They flocked to the towns, therefore, to join
those who had already escaped into industry, but finding that
factory life was even harder than village life, they tended at first
not to stay. In most districts, however, the backward methods of
agriculture proved less and less able to support the growing population, and soon the industrial employers found that they were in a
buyers' market so far as hiring labour was concerned. Between
1865 and 1890 the working-class population of the towns was
more than doubled, and in St Petersburg it increased, in forty
years, by twelve times.

The rate of growth of Russian industry was phenomenal—
higher than that of any other nation—and by 1900 Russia reached
fourth place in the world for industrial production. The capital
employed was mainly foreign, and many foreign firms started

their own enterprises—Ericsson, for instance, and Siemens, in St Petersburg. The State was also a great entrepreneur, banker, and financier, continuing a tendency started under Peter the Great and even earlier. But as an employer the Tsarist State was no better than the private capitalist. The Russian factory workers lived in the most degrading conditions; they endured in the eighties and nineties all the worst abuses of the early days of the Industrial Revolution elsewhere. Their miserable wages were often paid partly in kind, or on the 'tommy shop' basis, and they lived mostly in barracks, not merely as single men or single women but indiscriminately together, and if they raised a family they continued in the same barracks because there was nowhere else they could go.

'Nowhere, in all the factories in the province, is there any norm for accommodation of the workers in the barracks, which are huge, many-storeyed affairs with central corridors on each floor, and deal partitions not reaching up to the ceiling. They are packed to capacity, with less than two cubic yards of air space per man, and sometimes less than one cubic yard. Boards are provided to sleep on, very rarely anything in the way of a table or stool. Often the accommodation is in two tiers, the top tier being little more than two feet from the roof.'

This quotation is not taken from any Bolshevik source, but from the entry 'Factory Workers' in the *Brockhaus Encyclopaedia*, published (with the censor's permission) in St Petersburg in 1897. Figures under the same entry show that factory workers fed worse, on their poor wages, than a well-fed peasant. But what was a well-fed peasant? The standard of living was being depressed among the peasants too. They had to sell the corn, which they would have preferred to eat, in order to pay redemption dues and government taxes. In 1885 a Russian medical congress declared that: 'The primary cause of this frightful mortality (36 per thousand) is deficiency of bread. It is obvious that the reduction of one-seventh in the peasant's consumption

of bread during the last twenty years, as is shown by the computa-
tion of corn exports and corn production, has not come out of the
people's superfluities, but is literally wrung from their necessities.'

Once Russia became industrialized, the relative significance of
St Petersburg began to change. Since all other cities were becoming industrialized too, they were to that extent (if no other) all
becoming Europeanized. There was plenty of money made in
St Petersburg, but there was money made in every other city
too, and the exuberant speculators who lit their cigars with
twenty-five-rouble notes were as content to buy their way in the
society of Moscow, Kiev, Odessa, or Samara, as in St Petersburg, where they were bound to be much more looked down
upon. Moscow among other things had become the natural centre
for the railway system, and this emphasized the more remote
situation of St Petersburg. The money was not all in the hands of
boors, either. Moscow had the millionaire Morozov, who financed
the Moscow Art Theatre and bought Impressionist pictures, to set
against St Petersburg's millionaire Mamontov, who financed the
operas of Rimsky-Korsakov and Moussorgsky, and helped
Chaliapin after he had been dismissed from the conventional
Marinsky Theatre. Moscow had had a lively intellectual life of its
own for some time, and was felt to be freer than St Petersburg
where, because it was the capital, the powers of the Third Section
were more concentrated. Chekhov's Three Sisters yearned for
Moscow, not St Petersburg, where they no doubt knew they
would have been made to feel more provincial and dowdy, and
Moscow seemed to them, as it did to Chekhov, alive and brilliant
enough. It was characteristic of Tolstoy too that he turned his
back on the expensive, sophisticated life of St Petersburg fairly
early, and set up his workshop and press in Moscow, rejecting
both the Tsarist State and the reformers who wanted to use the
power of any kind of State. In short, the special, artificial position
of St Petersburg as the ill-placed centre of an out-moded system
was becoming emphasized more and more.

There is no space here to describe the reformist and revolutionary groups and movements which grew up—the Populists, 'Land
and Liberty', the Anarchists, the Nihilists, the National Will, the
Social Revolutionaries . . . some of them in the drawing-rooms
of idealist members of the middle and upper classes, some of them
in the stinking back streets of St Petersburg, among noisome
wooden houses and filth such as one reads of in *Crime and Punishment*. (Dostoevsky is the author above all others for nineteenth-
century St Petersburg.) The great dividing line which appeared,
as the groups grew more realistic, was between those who believed
they must seek the support of the peasants and the minority who
believed that only a movement based on the industrial workers
could succeed. Even as late as 1914 there were only five million
industrial workers, against perhaps six times as many working
peasants. But the peasants were scattered, usually though not
always backward, and jealously attached to their bits of land, and
they did not take kindly to propagandists from the towns, whom
they sometimes handed over to the police. They did have a promising tradition of revolt, however, because while they were serfs
they had never forgotten the free state which their ancestors had
enjoyed only a few hundred years earlier, before serfdom began.
The serfs had revolted many times on a large scale, and continuously, but sporadically, they burnt down landlords' houses. Many
an Oblomov, idling in St Petersburg, and hoping his bailiff would
send him a few thousand roubles, received news of fire and
plunder instead. In the last sixteen years before the Liberation
there were 800 peasant outbreaks which were large enough to
need suppression by the military, and after the Liberation these
did not cease. But they were local, not usually political in
character.

The industrial workers came from the peasantry, and over
Russia in general it was not always easy to say who was peasant
and who was town worker; they interchanged the roles a lot, and
a large proportion of industrial workers owned strips of land in

their original village and slipped back to help with the harvest
and so forth. The St Petersburg working class, however, like so
many other features of St Petersburg, was rather different. It was
the oldest, the most concentrated, and the most advanced group
of workers in Russia. Whereas as late as 1918 40 per cent of Moscow workers still had ties with villages, in St Petersburg the
figure was only 16½ per cent. Russia had become noted for the
large size of its industrial enterprises, and this was particularly
true of the capital, where in 1914 70 per cent of them employed
more than 500 workers apiece. The industrial workers,
for all their poverty, were acquiring a little education, and
in 1897, 75 per cent of St Petersburg workers could read and
write, against an average of 59 per cent for town workers as a
whole. There were second and third generation town workers
in St Petersburg now; they had no use for patriarchal ways de-
rived from the village, and they were beginning to understand
their miseries in both economic and political terms. At the
same time, they hadn't lost the brotherly solidarity of the
village, the great Russian capacity for acting together without
prearrangement in an emergency—and this could frequently
mean action against authority. (They had no experience of
participating in authority, but few Russians have ever had
that.)

Strikes were illegal, yet they took place. Trade unions were
illegal too before 1906, apart from the 'Zubatov' unions which
were deliberately organized by police agents, and known to be so
organized. Round about the turn of the century there were repeated famines, and several peasant risings in consequence. The
police-minded ministers of Alexander III and Nicholas II—nearly
all of them men of no capacity—responded by further repression
and by cutting down the local electoral rights which had been
granted not many years before. There was an increasing social
tension, felt by all classes, which burst right asunder, over the
whole of the Russian Empire, in the revolutionary year of 1905,

when Russia was being defeated in her stupid and ill-managed war with Japan.

But before this a small movement had begun, largely in St Petersburg, which broke with the tradition of other Russian movements. The inspiration came from the West, from Karl Marx. The Marxist parties (principally the Social Democrats) argued (to condense briefly and crudely) that capitalism was bound to dig its own grave, and that the industrial workers, who would be ground down more and more, must necessarily be in the end the leaders of a popular revolution, though in Russia there would first have to be a 'bourgeois' revolution to remove the Tsarist tyranny. Plekhanov, of whom a sentimental statue stands outside the Technical Institute in Leningrad, was the first Marxist leader, but he was soon overshadowed by Vladimir Ilyitch Ulianov, universally known by his 'underground' name of Lenin. If ever there was a revolutionary of genius it was Lenin. In 1903 he won a majority at the Congress of the Social Democratic Party, for his policy of a concentrated revolutionary organization, and the Party split into Bolsheviks and Mensheviks ('Majority' and 'Minority' parties). In a police State like Russia it was useless, he said, to have liberal ideas about free discussion in all the branches of a party, with mass support; nothing could be easier for the police to penetrate. The Bolshevik Party must be a small, selected, tightly disciplined body of whole-time, professional revolutionaries working in small cells, who at the right moment would be able to lead the masses, since the workers by themselves could not rise above what he called 'trade union consciousness', i.e. fighting for short-term economic advantage. In Russia such a party had to work underground, but in the uprisings of 1905 the Bolsheviks in many places took the lead. This kind of organization took most of the 'Democracy' out of 'Social Democracy', and later the Bolsheviks dropped the name 'Social Democratic Party' in order to dissociate themselves from the Western Social Democratic parties who hoped to achieve socialism by non-revolutionary means, and they began to call themselves Communists. The Mensheviks, although a minority at the Party Congresses (which had to meet outside Russia) actually had more support inside the country than the Bolsheviks until the October Revolution.

The near-revolution of 1905 was sparked off in St Petersburg by the massacre of 'Bloody Sunday', when 150,000 people marched to the Winter Palace, peacefully and unarmed, to present a petition to the Tsar asking for constitutional freedoms. They were headed by one Father Gapon, the leader of a 'police' union, who was later killed by enraged workers. The Tsar was not at the Palace, his officers gave orders to fire repeatedly on the crowd, and about a thousand were killed. A wave of shocked indignation ran round Europe, and within a few days half a million men were on strike in Russia. During the year three million workers came out on strike, for both political and economic demands, and there were mutinies in many Army units and in some ships of the Navy, including the famous battleship *Potemkin*—the subject of Eisenstein's film. Some of the workers' demands had to be granted, and Nicholas II was obliged to yield, in principle, some constitutional freedoms and a sort of parliament, the Duma. The workers had been poorly organized, but they acquired considerable revolutionary experience. In many places, including St Petersburg, workers or soldiers had set up their own *ad hoc* committees, which they called by the ordinary Russian word for a council—*soviet*. These popular committees were reborn when revolution broke out in 1917, and the name has been transferred to the formal governing bodies, 'elected' without choice of candidate, which exist in the Soviet Union today.

Widespread though the near-revolution had been, it did not seem that such an ill-organized bundle of rebellions could overthrow the autocracy, and from 1906 there was more repression, leaders (including Trotsky) were imprisoned or in exile, and workers' movements were scattered and weak. Yet for all this, nothing was quite the same as it had been before 1905.

In the first place there was the Duma. It was based on a franchise heavily weighted in favour of the well-to-do, and it was allowed no power over ministers, who were to remain responsible only to the Tsar. It was intended to be little more than a talking-shop. But as soon as it had met, in the Tavrida Palace, members of nearly all the twenty-six parties (liberals or moderates for the most part), presented a barrage of demands, including the confiscation of large estates, a democratic electoral system, the resignation of the existing Government, and the responsibility of future ministers to the Duma. Nicholas and his Government found this intolerable, and dissolved the Duma by force after only ten weeks. The Second Duma met with the same fate, and the Third Duma was then elected on such a narrow electoral basis that it contained a majority of docile conservatives.

Nicholas II, it seemed, was intent on destroying his own throne. With the obstinacy of a weak man, he went back on the promises he had been obliged to make in 1905, and sacked the very able minister, Witte, who had advised him. To the peasants the Tsar—any Tsar—had traditionally been a kind of Providence, an abstraction, a personification of justice; but this sort of charisma had been wearing very thin. Everyone now knew that Nicholas had promised freedom of speech and of assembly, and yet all over Russia peasants were being assaulted and killed by police and Cossacks for making use of these rights. An American journalist, William English Walling, was photographing a village in 1907:

... when some village women asked what I was doing. On explaining that I was going to use the picture to describe the village to foreigners, they shouted out in a tone of bitter irony. 'If you go back to Petersburg, show your picture to the White Tsar and let him see how we live—like dogs.' A passing peasant said: 'See what the Tsar has brought us to! He helps the landlords when they are in trouble, for us he does nothing. He did away with the Duma and the liberty he had granted us.' One peasant, when told of the dissolution of the Duma and the creation of the 'landlords' Duma', cried out 'What a crook!' What is interesting in these expressions is not only that they were new, but that they were said openly before perfect strangers. Certainly they have got a long way from the old belief in the 'God-given powers of the Tsar.'*

Walling went on to describe how much some peasants were reading and studying, and when he met the St Petersburg workers he was one of the very few foreign observers—perhaps the only one—to pick out Lenin, as early as 1907, as the most popular leader by repute. In spite of repressive methods, the temper of the people, it seemed, could not be repressed. The workers' movements began to revive, and in the first six months of 1914 there were over four thousand strikes.

During these years of civil turmoil, St Petersburg became a brilliant international centre of the arts, to a large extent through the personality of Diaghilev. He had no creative gift himself but his masterly, not to say masterful, gifts of organization and persuasion have ensured that his name still calls up for us in one word the primitive flavours of Stravinsky and Roerich, the barbaric Polovtsian Dances, the flat, almost Greek designs of Bakst, and the formalized folk themes of Goncharova, weighed down with interwoven ornament, as in *The Firebird*, for which Diaghilev commissioned Stravinsky to write the music in 1909. The *Mir Iskusstva* (World of Art) group around Diaghilev and Alexander Benois, through their magazine and their exhibitions, brought a large new public, in Russia as well as abroad, to appreciate not only modern but nineteenth-century Russian art—particularly the paintings of the great Repin, whose country house is now a museum just outside Leningrad. In the concert halls the latest works of Scriabin, Rachmaninov, and Medtner were played to enraptured audiences. Prokofiev was beginning; his 2nd piano concerto, performed in 1913, was dismissed as 'an insult' by most of the critics. Young people were divided into passionate followers of the two leading composers (according to Mr Herbert Swann, whose youth

* *Russia's Message*, 1908.

was spent among the St Petersburg *bourgeoisie*), so that when new partners met at a dance the first thing they said was 'Are you a Scriabinist or a Rachmanist?' The great poet Blok was outstanding among the Symbolists and later celebrated the Revolution in his remarkable poem *The Twelve*. Another Symbolist poet, Akhmatova, survived through much sorrow and persecution to our own day. World-famous artists, such as Nijinsky, Karsavina, Pavlova, and Chaliapin were coming to the height of their powers. In the theatre Meyerhold was astonishing the world with his futurist presentations of both classical and modern plays.

There was a fairly large cultured middle class now, and like the upper class, it was divided in its political sympathies. (Another Scriabin, cousin of the composer, had taken the name of Molotov and was doing underground work in the Bolshevik Party.) Some nobles were leaders of liberal opinion, but a large group, including many in the Government, resembled nothing so much as a bunch of eighteenth-century aristo's, responsible to no one—men such as that Minister of the Interior, for instance, who used to appear at private parties wearing a carnation in his flybuttons. Their wives accused the Empress, quite unjustly, of going to bed with Rasputin—no doubt because so many of them had been to bed with him already.

If the First World War had not taken place, Russia might perhaps have stumbled on to a more prosperous state. Education was growing fast, and her wealth was increasing at a prodigious pace in the last few years before 1914. Possibly, given time, more of this wealth could have filtered down to the ordinary population, as in Western countries, while a hard, independent, French-style peasantry, encouraged by the reforms of Stolypin, might have broken up the big estates by sheer economic pressure. In these two ways civil strife might have been diminished, though it would certainly not have disappeared. It is all a very big 'might have been', and it would certainly have had to be accompanied by the removal—probably by murder—of Nicholas II and some of his

Ministers, so that some more enlightened persons could have established a modicum of governmental institutions appropriate to the twentieth century.

But once Russia was involved in the war and brought to such a state of misery and chaos, it is impossible to believe that a revolution could have been avoided. It was bound to begin in St Petersburg as the seat of government, but whether it was to stop at the granting of representative institutions, or to be converted into a full Communist revolution against the institutions of property, depended upon the existence of the small, well-organized Bolshevik Party and above all upon the presence of the man of destiny, Lenin.

In 1914 Russia plunged into war with the same enthusiasm as the countries of Western Europe, and in a wave of anti-German feeling the name of the capital was at last russified into 'Petrograd'. The Russian campaign in East Prussia helped to relieve the pressure on Paris, and in 1916 General Brussilov's overwhelming victory over the Austro-Hungarian armies brought much relief to the Western Allies. (Brussilov later became a general in the Red Army.) But otherwise the war was for Russians a story of mounting suffering, appalling leadership, breakdowns, and corruption. Soldiers often hadn't a rifle apiece, boots, maps, food and the most elementary supplies were lacking, and from home there came news of food shortages, rising prices, profiteers flaunting in Petrograd, increasing civil chaos, and the complete incompetence of the Tsar and his staff. In Petrograd there were repeated strikes and food riots, prisoners were freed, and Army units refused to fire on mutineers. The Duma, conservative though its members were, was all against the Tsar, and in March, when even the imperial guard was deserting him, he was forced to abdicate. A Provisional Government was formed by some members of the Duma, under Kerensky, a Social Revolutionary (which means he was not very far to the Left), and they promised free elections for a constituent assembly. The March Revolution was

A life-size figure of Peter the Great in the Hermitage
Museum

The Winter Palace, now part of the Hermitage Museum

(*Below*) The main staircase inside the Hermitage

(*Above, left*) Natasha Kuchinskaya, a Leningrad student, is a Soviet champion in gymnastics

(*Below, left*) A patrol of workers from the Admiralty shipyard during the siege of Leningrad

(*Above*) Russian visitors to Lenin's room in the Smolny – his headquarters in 1917

(*Below*) On a quayside in Leningrad

'The Bronze Horseman' – Peter the Great – Leningrad's finest statue and the subject of Pushkin's finest poem

The Cameron Gallery of Catherine the Great's
Palace at Tsarskoe Selo – the masterpiece of the
Scottish architect Charles Cameron

The cascades and palace at Peterhof

The 'Upper Bath House' by the lake at Tsarskoe Selo

universally welcomed by the Western Powers, who hoped for an improved Russian military effort. But the Petrograd workers mistrusted the new Government from the start, and set up their own Soviet again. The same happened in other cities, and soldiers and sailors refused to obey their officers and formed Soviets too, while in the countryside the peasants waited for no new measures but took all the land for themselves. The Bolshevik Party was now operating openly, with its headquarters in the mansion of the prima ballerina Kshesinskaya, formerly mistress of the Tsar. (Her Art Nouveau mansion is still on view, and Kshesinskaya herself is still alive in Paris.)

To do justice to the events between the March and the November Revolutions is only possible within the covers of a large book; it was one of those periods when 'history' moves at its fastest. It is basically the story of vacillation by the Provisional Government and of mounting Bolshevik power. Soon after the March Revolution Lenin returned from exile to a thunderous welcome at the Finland Station, and as early as April he demanded that the Bolsheviks should go all out for a policy of opposition to the Provisional Government, nationalization of the land, power for the Soviets, and controlling power for the Bolsheviks in the Soviets. It was an audacious and apparently ridiculous programme at the time, since the Bolsheviks were still comparatively weak. Yet Lenin's gifts of oratory and analysis, the papers that poured from his pen, and the general march of events had within a few weeks converted the Party to his famous slogan 'All Power to the Soviets!' He was, says the eyewitness John Reed in *Ten Days That Shook The World*: 'Unimpressive, to be the idol of a mob, loved and revered as perhaps few leaders in history have been. . . . colourless, humourless, uncompromising and detached, without picturesque idiosyncrasies—but with the power of explaining profound ideas in simple terms, of analysing a concrete situation.'

In July there was an abortive rising from the Left; it was not

E

started by the Bolsheviks but Lenin had to flee to Finland. Now the commander-in-chief, Kornilov, tried to bring off a military coup from the Right. He failed dismally, the railwaymen tore up the lines in front of him, and his troops melted away. A week later the Bolsheviks had control of the Petrograd Soviet and had enormously increased their following everywhere. The moment for seizing power seemed near, and it was fixed for the night of November 6th–7th. Well planned in the headquarters at Smolny, with Trotsky in charge of actual operations, the November Revolution took the Winter Palace and all the strategic points in the city with only a few casualties on either side. (Other citizens were at the theatres the same night, applauding Chaliapin and Karsavina.)

The Provisional Government fell because it failed to take a decision on the only two issues that mattered to the people— the land, all the land, for the peasants, at any price, and peace for the nation, also at any price. The working population of Petrograd—and of Moscow and other places—believed the Bolsheviks meant business on these two issues, and no other party or authority looked like doing so. (Actually the Government signed decrees on these two crucial matters a few days before the November coup, but no one paid any attention to them by then.) Lenin read out decrees on 8th November which nationalized all private property in land and all mineral wealth, without compensation, and in March 1918, at the cost of an enormous sacrifice of territory, he was able to sign the Peace of Brest-Litovsk with Germany. (Among minor reforms he brought the calendar into line with that of other countries—which explains why the two Revolutions are referred to, in the old terms, as the Revolutions of February and October.)

To many citizens of Petrograd, looking back some years later, 'the Revolution' must have featured less as the events of 7th November than as the long, chaotic, usually grey period which came after. During these years, however, there was enthusiastic expansion of education, health services, and good entertainment for the masses, even through all the shortages of food, clothing, and every necessity. A huge fund of every kind of undeveloped talent was found among the peasants and workers—naturally enough, since they constituted over 90 per cent of the population. For many of the creative intelligentsia the first years were like a dawn of unlimited promise: artists were to become integrated members of society, it seemed, at last. The poetry of Yesenin, the stories of Babel, the declamatory verse of Mayakovsky, the startling new posters and designs of the 'Constructivists', not to mention the early paintings of Kandinsky and Chagall and the sculptures of Gabo, excited admiration far beyond the boundaries of Soviet Russia. But this movement was not allowed to last: the Constructivists had to produce more conventional work in order to survive; Kandinsky, Chagall and Gabo went abroad; and Yesenin and Mayakovsky committed suicide, though their works have mostly remained in favour. Before long Stalin had imposed the unimaginative monotony of 'Socialist Realism' in all fields.

From 1918 to 1920 the Civil War and the intervention by foreign powers had to be repulsed by the new Red Army organized by Trotsky. (One of its recruits from Petrograd was a young man called Kosygin.) Party dictatorship, and dictatorship inside the Party, became established very early, in spite of the warnings of Trotsky, Bukharin and others. There was a considerable revolt at Kronstadt in 1921, when sailors and workers and peasants, demanding an end to Bolshevik dictatorship and more independence for 'the small man', raised the banner of 'Soviets Without Communists', and were mown down by armed forces of their own kind. After this not only were all parties other than the Communist Party forbidden, but even the formation of 'fractions' inside the Party. This probably seemed reasonable to a great number of the sincere, rather crude, honest, often trigger-happy, basically goodhearted workmen who had pinned their faith on Lenin and the Bolsheviks—yet later this did not save many of their lives in the purges.

In March 1918 Lenin moved the capital to Moscow, partly in order to emphasize the break with all old traditions, partly because Moscow is a much more natural centre. Henceforth Peter's city ceased to be a determining force in Russian history, although it still holds a position of some special influence. Lenin laid the foundations of the Soviet State in Moscow, and there are those who say that when he died in 1924 it was Moscow which should have been renamed Leningrad.

What the people of Leningrad endured after 1918, what they shared in enthusiasms and in hopes bitterly disappointed, in the universal butchery of Stalin's purges, in the building up of education, and health, and the beginnings, in spite of all, of some material happiness—in all this their story has been barely different from that of the rest of the Soviet people, different only by virtue of their cultural inheritance, which even Stalin did not try to destroy.

But when the Second World War broke, one more bitter, heroic chapter was added to their history. In the two-and-a-half years' siege of Leningrad 750,000 people died, mostly from starvation. The city was without light, except in a few factories which managed to stay at work, it was without transport, and without fuel except what could be improvised by such means as crowding people from two blocks of flats into one, and burning all the timber in the other. Across the ice of Lake Ladoga lorries brought a precarious ribbon of supplies, but rations fell until those who were at work had to exist on half a pound of bread a day, and others on a quarter of a pound, with often no other rations at all. People ate dogs, cats, machine oil, paperhangers' paste. Those who were strong enough to bury the corpses received extra rations, otherwise in winter corpses often lay unburied for weeks.

The shells and bombs fell irregularly; there is still a notice preserved on the south side of the Nevsky, warning citizens to stay on that side when the sirens blew, because all attacks came from the south. One theatre company remained, playing to packed houses in an unheated theatre, its members so wan they could hardly stand. And it was typical of the independence of Leningrad that the staff of the Genetics Institute preserved the huge collection of rare grains which they might have eaten; it had been assembled by the great biologist N. I. Vavilov, who was at that time dying in a labour camp, all his work suppressed under a ban of Stalin's.

The Government recognized the heroism of Leningrad by awarding the city the highest decoration, the Order of Lenin, and one of the city's most gifted sons, Shostakovitch, composed his Seventh Symphony in honour of the bitter time.

Today, if you ask a taxi-driver—for preference an elderly taxi-driver—to show you the sights of Leningrad he will respond with typical Leningrad courtesy, he will drive you along the Nevsky to the Admiralty and the Winter Palace, will ignore most of the other classical beauties, though pointing out the Peter–Paul fortress because of its honourable list of prisoners, and he will then, with pride, take you on a tour of places, mostly undistinguished in appearance, which were key spots in the Revolution or in the work of Lenin. That is his city. He is not a Party member, he is just a survivor of that robust, raw working-class that helped to make the Revolution.

If it is a warm afternoon you probably notice as you drive along the Nevsky, or maybe take tea there in the Café Sever, an old, distinguished-looking lady who has survived it all and come through. She has probably worked at something on the fringes of the academic or artistic world; her grandchildren are probably doing electronic calculations or doctoring in Siberia; she still lives, perhaps, in one room of the mansion where as a little girl she wore French dresses and looked forward to glamorous balls in the Tavrida Palace; no one objects to her old-fashioned clothes; she is likely, indeed, to be respected and loved; she is able, sometimes, to forget the unbearable *cortège* which her life has been—the executions, the arrests, and the fading into death from starvation. She is a symbol, not quite all sad and grey, along with the taxi-driver, of the old-in-the-new city on the Neva.

Chapter 4

Leningrad Today

TODAY Leningrad is the second largest city in the Soviet Union, the greatest port, and the second greatest industrial centre, accounting for 10 per cent of the country's output. It disputes cultural and academic supremacy with Moscow, and its pre-eminence as the most beautiful city in the USSR is unquestioned.

It is commonly regarded as the next best city to live in after Moscow, and some would put it higher. One of the clauses in the punishment of political offenders involves their exclusion from residence in major cities; the first stage is the prohibition of residence in Moscow and Leningrad.

A woman journalist in Moscow lamented to me that she wished her husband would get a job in Leningrad, 'but it would mean something less important than what he does here. I enjoy my own work here, but Moscow is like a madhouse to live in—all this rushing around to see some central authority or other and getting in the right queue, all this tearing up of roads and building of flyovers and underpasses—right in the centre of the city they never seem to stop pulling down and rebuilding—and all these millions of people who aren't Muscovites and who don't know our city—it's always full of tourists and people from the provinces on official *komandirovka*, and grubby peasant traders all the way up from Georgia. . . .

'When my brother was released from Stalin's labour camp—he slaved seven years on the hydroelectric station at Bratsk—he went back to his old profession and the Journalists' Union looked after him and gave him preferential treatment—along with all the others!—but what he wanted above all was to go and live in

Leningrad. He couldn't stand the pace of Moscow any more. Leningrad is so much more *tikhy*—the dictionary only says *tikhy* means "quiet", but you know we use it for a dozen more meanings, like—*convenience,* I think—and *elbowroom*—and enough time to show good manners—and even common sense!'

It is only fair to add that people from smaller towns complain about the strain and bustle of life in Leningrad, but almost everyone agrees that life seems to run more smoothly there than in Moscow. Mainly, one feels, this is because of an enormous sense of pride in the city where the Revolution was made, the heroic city which has risen again immaculate after the siege. It is a sense which seems to infect the new population—originally from the Baltic Republics, the Volga, the Ukraine, or even Armenia—who nowadays outnumber the hereditary inhabitants of Leningrad. The courtesy of the city, in comparison with Moscow, strikes you as soon as you come out of the station. It is partly a generous old Russian sense of brotherhood and partly something more sophisticated, a sense that it is more rational and humane to push and shove a bit less, and not cold-shoulder the stranger. In fact when you ask the way in Leningrad, people will not only tell you, they will often walk all the way with you. By English standards there is indeed a good deal of pushing and shoving, but by and large the city leaves one with a more civilized impression: the old sense of the behaviour appropriate to a great capital, even something of a 'European' sense, one could say, is still to be felt, and it has received a fresh impulse from the historic status which the city now has, not merely for a cultured minority but for every one of its citizens.

The demotion of Leningrad to second place has probably strengthened their pride and has also made it easier for them to substantiate that pride; they have no need to run so fast to keep up as the Muscovites do. Moscow has all the place-seeking and intrigue of a Washington, combined with the labyrinthine obstacles of an intermeshed and stonewalling central bureaucracy.

Leningrad has its local bureaucracy, of course, just like Moscow city and every other Soviet city, but it does not have the same load of central Government and Party *apparatchiks* as the capital has. Perhaps this is why in Leningrad one sees less of the new Soviet *bourgeoisie*—the well-fed men in square-shouldered suits and very wide trousers whose existence is constructed around toeing the line and seeing that others toe it.

The Leningraders naturally have to endure the same restrictions as other Soviet citizens—the obligatory meetings and unanimous resolutions at their place of work, the queues for all but the simplest goods and services, the censorship of newspapers, magazines, and books both new and secondhand, the ban or almost complete ban on foreign travel, the throttling delays for passes and permissions in order to undertake what is, in many other countries, automatically free and unquestioned, and the black market and *blat*, or corrupt practices, in order to short-circuit these delays. Before the great siege they had to endure the purges of the nineteen-thirties, and after the siege they had to endure the purges of Stalin's later paranoia, when, as Khrushchev said to the Twentieth Party Congress in 1956: 'Many thousands of honest and innocent Communists died as a result of the fact that all kinds of slanderous "confessions" were accepted, and as a result of forcing accusations against oneself and others.'

Khrushchev was speaking to a Congress of Communist Party members, but the 'honest and innocent' who died were far from being only Party members. In Leningrad the hand of Stalin fell even more heavily than elsewhere, for the whole wave of terror began, apparently, as a result of the murder of Kirov, the Leningrad Party chief, in December 1934. He was murdered by a dissident Communist, and it is sometimes suggested that the murder may have been engineered in order to provide an excuse for beginning the terror. Be that as it may, Leningrad was naturally full of men and women who had helped to make the Revolution, and whose capacity for independent action and thought now seemed dangerous. It was they in particular who were the target for the arrests and executions by the NKVD (the National Commissariat for Internal Affairs). And the NKVD, as two ex-prisoners have said, '. . . lived in terror of the Special Department, the members of which themselves lived in terror of a change in their superiors, which would bring about their downfall.'* It was only the old, natural, tacit, peasant solidarity which supported Russians through the worst years, and which was sometimes able to render life in labour camps less grim.

Those times have gone, but the Party has continued to keep one of its harsher officials installed as Party Secretary in Leningrad, in order to keep a sharp eye on the city which enjoys such unique traditions and potentialities. During both the purges the Secretary was Zhdanov, a great enemy of innovation and experiment in the arts, and again, in the later nineteen-sixties, the theatres and cultural life of Leningrad felt a repressive hand (though less heavy than Zhdanov's) some time before the new restrictive line spread, in 1967–8, to Moscow and the country at large. The intellectuals of Leningrad are experienced in these matters; in times like the present they wait for the next wave of relaxation, and they exercise their wit; it was probably Leningrad that invented the phrase which Russians use when there is a sudden awkward pause in conversation: instead of 'An angel is passing over', Russians say, 'A policeman is being born'.

It would be an elementary mistake, however, to assume, because they are so often mishandled and held down by their Government, that Russians—even sophisticated Russians—must be opposed to 'their Government' all round. They may object to the privileges enjoyed by a few, they will certainly grumble at the frequent delays and breakdowns and at stupid planning and bureaucracy and inefficiency, and they may prefer not to take any part in the work of the clumsy political machine. (An English student at Leningrad University, Harvey Pitcher, found that nearly all the

* F. Beck & W. Godin, *Russian Purge*, 1951.

'activists' in the university were students who came from the villages.) But 'the Government' operates through agencies which are too numerous and too various for them often to be thought of collectively, in the way that outsiders think of them, as simply 'the system'.

It is 'the Government', for instance, ultimately, through a great number of ministries and departments, which has made the Leningrad Elektrosila enterprise into the biggest electrical engineering concern in the country; which employs half the population of Leningrad in the engineering, metalworking and shipbuilding industries, and another quarter in the textile and light industries; which has built up in Leningrad the biggest rubber factory in Europe; which has provided enterprises such as Elektrosila or the Kirov Works (the old Putilov Works) with plentiful research and technological staff; and which has stimulated the growth of Leningrad's heavy industry so that by 1940 its output was twelve times what it was in 1913, and in 1955 it was nearly twenty-nine times the pre-revolutionary figure. It is, ultimately, through 'Government' agencies that the people who live in the new avenues and suburbs nowadays build Atlantic liners and make automatized machine tools, generators with a capacity of 100,000 kilowatts and more, giant travelling cranes, electronic devices in hundreds of kinds, and millions of miles of nylon fibre —to quote only a few of Leningrad's products.

It is another arm of 'the Government', ultimately, which has multiplied the hospitals and provided such a health service that Leningrad now has one doctor for every 200 of the population, where in 1913 there was only one for every 914. (Old St Petersburg was surprisingly lavish with statistics.) It would be unsafe to say how many all-purpose schools Government has provided, since their number grows continually—over 500, at least, for a population of three million, besides about fifty institutions of higher education, including the university, and the Mining Institute founded under Catherine the Great.

It is the Leningrad City Soviet which is building a hundred new
flats every day and has built the Leningrad Metro, through extremely difficult swampy or clay soil, and made its stations glitter
with marble and granite and aluminium and glass. The new flats
are not often large by British standards—two fair-sized rooms
most usually, with kitchen, bath, and a large hall for parking of
winter clothes and boots and stores. But lighting and central
heating are included in the very modest rent, and the flats are a
great improvement on the old wooden houses, which have now
all but disappeared. They are an improvement too, on some of the
solider older apartments: one has only to turn into one of the
gloomy courtyards of the old city to see how shabbily people can
be housed, even at a fashionable address such as Nevsky Prospect or the Moika Embankment. The finance for all the new pro-
jects is Government finance, since local Soviets are assigned all
their revenue from the national budget, but it is the Leningrad
touch which has made them less monotonous or pretentious than
similar developments in other Soviet cities, so many of which are
becoming indistinguishable from one another, all the way from
Murmansk to Vladivostok.

The memorial to those who fell in the Revolution, for instance,
is so unassuming in its dignity that it can easily be overlooked by
visitors, especially if they do not understand Russian. It is in
Mars Field (Marsovo Polye), the great open space overlooked by
the Marble Palace, the Engineers' Castle, and the former Pavlovsky
Barracks. Formerly a dusty parade ground, and the scene of many
workers' demonstrations, after November 1917 it was made into
the green park it is today, with low walls and low granite blocks,
as quiet as something in ancient Greece, inscribed with epitaphs
in verse by Lunacharsky, the first Soviet Commissar of Education.

The new European architecture of the nineteen-twenties, de-
riving mostly from the Bauhaus, was at first regarded as eminently
suitable; it was revolutionary, like the USSR, and it had the ad-
vantages of being cheap and of lending itself to mass production.

However, the few buildings in Leningrad which were designed
under this influence are not good examples: the Kirov District
Palace of Culture, for instance, looks more like a German provincial railway station. This was an intellectual's view of what
was revolutionary; early in the nineteen-thirties it was ruthlessly
swept away by Stalin, along with Futurist poetry, the paintings and
designs of Malevitch, Tatlin, and Lissitsky, and every other mani-
festation of intellectual modernism. Bauhaus architecture was
insultingly bare and insultingly cheap; how could it express the
joy and pride of the victorious workers? They must have their
own exultant ornament and display. Fortunately Leningrad
escaped the most revolting excesses of Stalinist pseudo-pomp,
because its classical heritage was so very large and so respected,
so incorporated into the Soviet tradition. There was a revival of
classical features, therefore, and at first this was not often successful: Corinthian columns and pilasters appliquéd to a five or seven-
storey apartment block simply do not fit. But the Leningrad
architects now show more sensibility, and though there is still a
good deal of unnecessary copying, in the best modern buildings
the classical features are much more integrated, or transformed
with taste.

The most attractive designs are perhaps not outstanding examples of modern architecture, but they are at least pleasant—the
Kalinin Square, for instance, which shows a successful treatment
of an open space where three avenues meet. The 'Gigant' Cinema,
which is not gigantic, and has a smallish upper storey resting on a
broad lower colonnade, is set back and centred behind the tall
statue of President Kalinin, and centred also between five-storey
blocks recalling Renaissance Rome. On each side of the cinema
a broad tree-lined avenue leads away into the distance. Elsewhere
the classical rotunda has been revived, as in the modest Metro
station in the Victory Park (by Getskin and Shuvalov), where
modern metal and glass give a slenderer effect than anything in
the eighteenth century. The Young Spectators' Theatre, designed

by Zhuk, in a small park on Zagorodny Prospect, is an excellent
modern-style building of plain white verticals, between which one
looks into the great foyer which almost surrounds the building.
The auditorium itself is shallow, and has not only first-class visi-
bility from all the seats but first-class access to them as well. The
Kirov Stadium, in the Victory Park on the shore of the Gulf of
Finland, is a great oval of the most restrained and unembellished
appearance, in the middle of a huge green artificial mound. It
holds 80,000 spectators, and was designed by Nikolsky, Kashin,
and Stepanov.

But where, asks the tourist, is the war damage in Leningrad? It
seems an extraordinary question to ask after the shelling of two
and a half years, but there is practically none to be seen, except in
a few places on the outskirts which have been left as a memorial.
All the classical buildings have been restored so that the restora-
tions do not even look new. And the city architects took the
opportunity at the same time of pulling down some of the worst
nineteenth-century 'improvements' and restoring those streets
to their original design.

So the architecture of Leningrad taken as a whole today, like the
architecture of St Petersburg in the old days, can symbolize to a
great extent the contemporary character of the city. It illustrates
the mass growth and development, the political drive and the
control so often apparently unnecessary, and yet often unexpectedly yielding to respect and affection for the monuments of the
past. Foreigners strolling out of the main hotel, the Astoria, dis-
cover within a few yards an equestrian statue on a towering Kaiser
Wilhelm sort of plinth, flanked by female figures impersonating
Justice, Truth, Wisdom, and Strength. It faces, across the square,
the long sandstone building where the red flag flies continuously
—the seat of the city executive. It ought to be a statue of a Bolshevik hero, but the period is all wrong, and the visitors spell
out the name on the base incredulously: it is Nicholas I, the 'Tsar-
Gendarme'. And he does look like an officer of the gendarmerie

reviewing his troops; the guidebook is not just making propaganda when it contrasts the stiffness of his pose, his features, and his horse, with Leningrad's best statue, the soaring Bronze Horseman, created by Falconet to honour a much better Tsar. Peter the Great seems about to take off into a glorious future from the granite promontory on which he is poised facing the Neva, but the oppressor Nicholas, one would think, should long since have been removed, plinth and all. In Moscow his statue would probably have been melted down, but the old capital is a city which likes to feel more of one piece with its history. They have overcome their dark past and swept away all its worst features; something with pretensions to being a work of art can be preserved.

Similarly, after the Revolution the Nevsky Prospect was at first renamed the October Prospect, but most people continued to call it 'the Nevsky', and some years ago the old name was officially restored. Many of the natives, even the young, use other old names among themselves: the best food shop, officially 'Gastronom No. 1,' is referred to by the genuine Leningraders as 'Eliseyev's', recalling the days when it was an elegant store under that proprietorship. And there has been a small revival of some old Russian local colour which one might have thought beneath the dignity of Soviet attention. Troikas, for instance—the three-horsed sleighs with high horse-collars and jingling bells which are rarely seen in the countryside any more—are now provided for week-end rides in some of the parks. The city badly needs colour in winter. In February everyone is longing for a break, and as something of a substitute for the old Maslenitsa, or Shrovetide, a bit of a fair is held—a slight, formalized descendant of the old Maslenitsa which we know from Stravinsky's *Petrouchka*, and it is no longer held in the gardens right under the Admiralty spire as it used to be, but still it is something. It is at least something of brilliant colour. Red, poppy red, a dramatic assertion against the snow or against the green forest—that is the old

Russian colour, and with it there is the deep evening blue of the magician's tent in *Petrouchka,* the blue that is often used on Russian church domes: those are the basic Russian colours to be made sparkling with white and with stars of all the other colours, and they use them in the fair and they use them all the time for toys and packagings and matchboxes. (No country, surely, has such a variety of matchbox labels as Soviet Russia.) They do up their matches in gay dozens in these old designs, and in summer they sell them from stalls on the broad pavements down the Nevsky, along with secondhand books, and combs and cosmetics and little bowls.

In summer the Nevsky, the embankments and the Summer Garden are the places to promenade in, and there are 620 bridges (only fifteen fewer than in Amsterdam) to linger on, joining up Leningrad's nineteen islands and crossing its sixty-eight canals. The Neva still lies like a great lake in the centre, and you can ride it in hydrofoils or motor-boats, or you can join the queue for small boats, at the parks farther downstream, and sail or row out into the Gulf of Finland, looking back at Leningrad with the dome of St Isaac's appearing above it like a golden roc's egg. In winter almost everyone goes skiing, using the light birchwood Russian skis. Since the Winter War of 1940, when the Russians found themselves outskied by the Finns, the Soviet Government has encouraged skiing so much that it is now probably the most accessible sport.

The gayest occasions, naturally, are the two *Prazdniks,* the annual holidays for May Day and for Revolution Day on November 7th. Everyone gets two days' holiday, many people seem to manage four, and a custom of exchanging 'seasonal' presents (as well as at New Year) has grown up; some shops offer horribly expensive boxes of chocolates, cases of liqueurs in gaudy wrappings, and so forth, got up for the purpose. The trams are festooned with fairy lights, and among all the red flags there flutters the plain sky-blue flag which is the emblem of Leningrad—a symbol of the sea, and a rare distinction among Soviet regional flags, which are not usually allowed more than minor variations from the overriding Party red. The Prazdniks are 'governmental' occasions, but the processions are all over by lunch-time, and the slogans and portraits of the Politbureau are taken down soon afterwards. They are felt to be important national days, but masses of people no longer turn out for them; they watch the processions at home on the television, or go straight off into the country or to visit friends. Respect for the occasion of the holidays has not fallen away to the same extent as respect for the religious basis of Christmas and Easter has in Britain, but it is taken very much for granted. When Russians greet each other automatically at these times with 'Happy Holiday!' they are scarcely communicating more than we do when we say 'Merry Christmas!'

The University of Leningrad ranks equal, academically, with the University of Moscow, but socially it feels itself superior because it is the oldest university in Russia—it was founded in 1819—and because of its association with the old capital. The architecture again has something to do with it: Moscow University has nothing, in either its new skyscraper or its old building down town, to compare with the tremendous eighteenth-century corridor which runs along the four-hundred-yard frontage of the Leningrad University building. Everyone meets here, under the portraits and busts of famous alumni—writers such as Turgenev and Nekrasov—and great professors of the past—Mendeleyev, Dokuchayev, or A. A. Popov, who invented radio independently of Marconi. The University has academic staff in something like the proportion of 1400 to 11,000 students, besides several thousand who take courses by correspondence. They are serious students, and as in other Soviet universities, they are kept hard at work during their five years. They have no *avant-garde* magazines or societies (though there is some *avant-garde* private discussion), and they indulge in no demonstrations or sit-ins, nor would they be allowed to. But their individual sympathies and their social

F

life are warm; parties and dances are fairly frequent, usually on the basis of one of the hostels where they live.

They are far outnumbered by the students of the forty-odd higher institutions, some of which are counted higher than the university in certain specialities. The Herzen Teachers' College, for instance, behind the courtyard with the high grille on the Moika canal, is a university in itself, has almost as many students as the university, and teaches the English language to a standard acknowledged to be higher. I have heard language classes taught there with a refinement and accuracy which are rare in any British university, and which are almost unbelievable when one realizes that few of the teachers have ever visited an English-speaking country.

But delightful though so many of the students can be, their development is rather held back by their heavy syllabuses and their very limited grants, besides which growing up seems to take longer in Russia than in Britain. For a good sample of the educated young it might be better to look at some of the young professional people. Those who have money to spend may be found in Leningrad's few, and modest, cafés and dance places, or in the few restaurants—oriental ones for preference, or perhaps in one of the houseboat restaurants moored in the Neva, though the food there is not so good. But few of them haunt these places often; they also haunt the various professional and cultural clubs (by no means only the clubs associated with their own professions)—they haunt the Actors' Club, the Film Workers' Club, or the Writers' Club, when they can get in, and they particularly gather anywhere where they can hear foreign languages. The Teachers' Club, for example, produces plays in English, such as *Pygmalion* or *Time and the Conways*, and I am told that 'several cinemas' often show films in English, French, Italian or Spanish 'without subtitles'. It is significant that the backbone of this public for foreign culture seems to be largely composed of engineers and scientists. (At the university, too, it is engineers and scientists, as all-round personalities, who are said to form the greater part of the natural *élite* among students; arts specialists are regarded as a little inferior—too academic, perhaps.) On one occasion when I was invited to meet a couple of dozen members of the USSR–Great Britain Society 'to talk about Britain', almost everyone present, of either sex, was a practising engineer—and during our two-and-a-half hour session they wanted to hear about Norman Wisdom and Agatha Christie and George Mikes as well as about British education and the National Health Service.

It is not that these people feel near to Europe because they live in Leningrad. So far as the possibility of an actual visit is concerned they are no better placed than they might be if they lived two thousand miles away in Novosibirsk. Leningrad has 100,000 foreign visitors a year, it is true, and it sees regular parties of Finns, who seem to come mainly to get away from their own country's liquor laws: 'the first coachload of Finns is the first sign of spring', they say nowadays. There are Soviet sailors in the streets with black ribbons fluttering from their caps, foreign cruise ships occasionally anchor right by the city, and once a year there is a great gathering of shrewd visitors for the fur sales, but on the whole the 'window on Europe' has rather frosted glass in it today, so far as direct access for Russians is concerned. They are avid, however, for all the contact they can get; it is all part of the huge national appetite for—there is no word to use but the overworked word—for culture. Apply what sceptical tests you like, it is a genuine, humane, deepfelt, natural appetite, and Leningrad, by virtue of its traditions, its institutions and its unique atmosphere feels itself to have a special position and a special responsibility: though Moscow is a greater centre in the sense that more is going on, Leningrad likes to feel that in some ways it is still the cultural capital.

Soviet Russians, or a high proportion of them, are avid for culture, partly because they are brought up that way and partly because it is something which calls forth individual quality (and the overworked Russian word *kulturny* includes neat habits, politeness, and general considerateness as well as a taste for the arts). They have an appetite for culture also partly because it was something which until recently was accessible only to a privileged few, and also partly because classical works in all the arts are made so accessible, while there is a relative shortage of light entertainment. They feel a particular attraction for foreign things, and a particular attraction for the works of their own past, because there is a sense of exploration about both—and Leningrad can satisfy this more than anywhere else. They are impassioned by their own classics for two other reasons: because there is a more profound humanity in the great nineteenth-century Russian novels and Russian music than in all but a small number of Soviet works, and because their cultural past is such an immediate and limited past. Pushkin published his first poems in 1814, and before Pushkin there is not much that attracts ordinary readers today. There are still plenty of elderly Russians whose fathers knew Tolstoy or Chekhov or Tchaikovsky, and there are even a few very old people who knew them personally; the grandson of Dostoevsky works as an engineer in Leningrad; and even the links with Pushkin, the greatest of them all, are short. Miss E. M. Almedingen, who lives in England now, says in the introduction to her book, *She Married Pushkin*: 'Most people born in Russia learn to look upon Pushkin as an intimate member of their own household. Pushkin's poems, in particular his fairy tales and lyrics, were known and learnt by heart before the hard printed word came into its own in the nursery. . . . He was in the music, written by Russia's great composers, like Glinka. He was also in the humbly expressed artistry of Russian harvesters and boatmen. . . . My grandfather, Serge de Poltoratzky, himself a man of letters, was his intimate friend.'

The Russian Shakespeare, so to speak, could thus be the friend of an ancestor no more distant than her grandfather, for a woman

living in 1968. Far more is known and recorded about Pushkin
than about Shakespeare, and Leningrad is the repository of much
of that; all his manuscripts are preserved in the Institute of Russian
Literature, and the house on the Moika, where he died after his
duel with D'Anthès, is a Pushkin Museum. As for Glinka, there
are fourteen addresses where he lived, and there are similar relics,
not to mention statues and busts, of Tchaikovsky and Borodin, of
Dostoevsky and Gogol, and of almost every great composer and
writer of the nineteenth century.

Leningrad is still the greatest centre of book production in the
USSR; something like 200 million books a year issue from its
presses. The best bookshop in the country, particularly noted for
old books, is on the Nevsky Prospect, and the Saltykov–Shche-
drin Library (originally opened in 1814), is one of the world's
great libraries. Its twelve million volumes include a particularly
rich collection of oriental books, and it is well stocked with
books in European languages, including many of the most
recent.

It was Leningrad, I think, which started the Public Design
Bureau—an organization to help people choose furnishings and
furniture for their homes. It has 10,000 voluntary workers today,
and if it didn't start in Leningrad it must have started not far
away in Estonia, where so much of the good, Scandinavian-
type Soviet design comes from; it would then be Leningrad
which developed this counselling service on a wide scale.

Of Leningrad's greatest glories, the Kirov Ballet and the in-
credible Hermitage collection, I propose to say almost nothing;
each of them has been the subject of a book in English, weighing
seven or eight times as much as the present one. The Hermitage is
quite possibly the greatest art collection in the world; its two
million objects include thirty-eight Rembrandts, forty Rubens,
a Leonardo, a priceless collection of gold objects 2,500 years old,
and five or six rooms of Impressionist and Post-Impressionist
paintings. In earlier Soviet days I was directed to these modern

pictures grudgingly, and found them accompanied by 'explanations' of the most primitive and denigratory Marxist nature; now you have only to speak with a foreign accent and the attendants direct you upstairs before you can say 'Impressionists'. When you get to the galleries you find a knowledgable and pleasant woman giving the same sort of lecture as can be heard anywhere else in Europe. And there are twenty other museums in Leningrad, besides fifteen associated exclusively with Lenin, some of them consisting only of a single room where he once lived and worked.

The admirers of the Kirov Ballet argue fiercely with the devotees of the Moscow Bolshoi, and their loyalties can cut across local patriotism. Personally I somewhat prefer the Bolshoi company, but as a theatre I much prefer the intimate Cambridge blue and silver auditorium of the Kirov Theatre (the old Marinsky), with its many private-looking boxes and small refreshment rooms, to the over-large red plush hall of the Bolshoi Theatre. Other Leningrad theatres are also rather more intimate than the big Moscow theatres—the Comedy Theatre, for instance, where Akimov directed, and the Gorky Theatre of Tovstonogov, the leading director of the city since Akimov died. Tovstonogov is noted for his completely silver Volga car, a rare distinction in a country which does not much encourage flamboyance in the individual.

In fact the foreigner, at his first visit, is usually impressed by the absence of what he may consider to be striking individuals, or individuals of any outstanding class or type. The audiences at all the theatres, or the Russian visitors to the Hermitage, seem at first glance to be exactly the same sort of people as one finds filling the Kirov Stadium to watch football or motor racing, or at the circus or the ice show, or shopping or simply hanging about the suburban avenues and indulging in hooliganism—and Leningrad has quite as much hooliganism as other Soviet cities. But this is to judge, as one is accustomed to at home, by clothes and personal appearance and personal 'presence', and these tests can be very misleading when applied to Russians. The shining, neat young man may be a lorry driver, and the one in creased clothes and a frayed tie may be a university mathematician earning twice the lorry driver's salary. The old Russian communal-brotherly way does not foster the need for personal statement or self-assertion, and though it breeds some admirable virtues, it doesn't breed much of the kind of self-discipline and sense of individual responsibility which we are used to in the West. To explain this in full is impossible here (I have written the best part of another book about nothing else)* but it can perhaps be epitomized by two features of the Leningrad streets. In the first place they are extremely free from litter, like most Soviet streets. That was achieved largely as a communal affair, and if you drop a piece of paper today someone, not an official, is sure to remind you, politely but firmly, that it ought to go in the litter can. But on the other hand whenever it rains the pavements, even on the Nevsky, are full of puddles, because they are so unevenly laid. It was the responsibility of some individual to lay the asphalt smoothly and on a firm base, and he scamped it.

The main feature of the Soviet social scene today is that individuality of every kind, and in almost every sense of the word, is beginning to grow freely out of the old base. And although the Government fears many manifestations of it, such as the demand behind the scenes for free elections, the Government badly needs individual talent and a developed sense of individual responsibility in so many other ways; and the enormous growth in education, the better housing and the generally rising standard of living, which are the result of Government policy, have inevitably fostered these. Leningrad, more than anywhere except the special 'science towns', is the place to see this new flowering, and once the visitor knows some Russian and talks to a few Russians, he becomes able to distinguish better between persons, and to realize

* *Russians as People*, 1960.

how many intelligent, responsible, excellently well-mannered people there are, particularly among the young. (The exponents of the real Leningrad manner—a most impressive blend of the old and the new—could win international competitions against the best English public school products.)

It is hardly surprising that along with all this growing 'culture' there is some philistinism, but that seems to me also evidence of individualities developing, if only out of resentment about other individualities. When eventually there are more and better clothes to be had, more and better consumer goods of every kind—and the Soviet press admits there aren't enough yet—one would expect philistinism to decrease. Apart from a few very highly-placed people, there is not such a great difference between the everyday conditions of cultured people in the best jobs and the everyday conditions shared by everybody else: they all stand in the same queues, waste the same time in frustrated shopping, and chase up the same ways of circumventing the shortages of goods and skills. They all turn down their earflaps against the same winter, shuffle over the same icy streets, and pack into the same trams and buses, where it is your sovereign duty, if you sit by the window, to keep a little spyhole breathed upon and unfrozen so that you can tell your fellow-passengers where you have all got to. . . .

Whatever the burden of bureaucracy and censorship and police files and Party dictatorship, there can be no doubt that Leningrad is a far better provided city, better fed and more comfortable, for the totality of its inhabitants, than St Petersburg ever was. It is also cleaner—indeed a beautifully clean city. And it has simply ceased to merit the old, furious condemnation of Dostoevsky as 'the most abstract and artificial town there is'. That quality of the old capital has gone.

Soviet Russia is by no means a country in which I would choose to live permanently, but when I am there I go to Leningrad from Moscow with the same sort of exhilaration as I go, as often as I can, from London to Oxford or Cambridge—not for the museum aspect, the historico-architectural pageant, but for the concentration of intelligence and architecture and youth in a city which is neither metropolitan-hectic nor backwater-provincial, but brimming with life.

Index

Academy of Arts, 26, 29
Admiralty, 1, 9, 16, 34
Akhmatova, Anna, 51
Akimov, theatre director, 74
Alexander I, 32, 37, 59
Alexander II, 32, 38, 41–2
Alexander III, 42, 46
Alexander Nevsky monastery, 9, 16
Alexandrinsky Theatre, 34
Alexis, Tsarevitch, 14, 18
Anna, Empress, 18
Anthropological Museum, 15, 16

Babel, Isaak E., 55
Bakst, Léon, 38, 50
Ballet, 28, 38, 74
Benois, Alexandre, 38, 50
Blok, Aleksandr, 51
Bloody Sunday, 48
Bolsheviks, 47, 52, 53–4
Borodin, Alexander, 38, 73
Bourse, 9, 35
Boyars, 11
Brest-Litovsk Treaty, 54
Brussilov, General, 52
Bukharin, Nikolay, 55

Cameron, Charles, architect, 26, 30
Canals, 3, 30
Capitalism, 43
Catherine I, 11, 18
Catherine the Great, 25–8
  conquests, 25
  influence on culture, 26–7, 28
  repression, 28
Chagall, Marc, 55
Chaliapin, Feodor, 44, 51
Charles XII, 5, 7
Chekhov, Anton, 44
Communist Party, 62
Communists, 48, 55
Coronations, 11, 14

Dargomizhsky, Alexander, 32
Decembrists, 39
Diaghilev, Serge, 2, 50
Dokuchayev, V.V. scientist, 32, 69
Dostoevsky, Fëdor, 2, 33, 38, 40, 41, 44, 72, 73, 76
Duma, 30, 48, 49, 52

Elizabeth, Empress, 21, 25
Emancipation of serfs, 41–2
Evelyn, John, 13, 14

Fokine, Michel, 38
Fontanka canal, 10, 16

Gabo, Naum, 55
Gapon, Father, 48
Glinka, Mikhail, 32, 72, 73
Gogol, Nikolay, 32, 33, 40, 73
Goncharov, Ivan, writer, 41
Goncharova, Nathalie, designer, 50
Gostinny Dvor, 29
Griboyedov, Aleksandr, writer, 32
Griboyedov Canal, 38

Hare Island, 6, 17
Hermitage, 29, 37, 73-4
Herzen, Aleksandr, writer, 41
Herzen College, 70
Holidays, 68-9

Ingria, 4
Intelligentsia, 27
Ivan VI, 18
Izhory, tribe, 4

Kandinsky, Wassily, 55
Karenina, Anna, 1
Karsavina, Tamara, 1, 51
Kazan Cathedral, 35
Kerensky, Aleksandr, 10, 52
Khrushchev, Nikita, 61
Kirov, Sergey, 61
Kirov Ballet, 74
Kokorinov, architect, 29
Kornilov, Lavr, 54
Kosygin, Aleksei, 55

Kronstadt, 7, 55
Krylov, Ivan, 32
Kshesinskaya, Mathilde, 53

Lake Ladoga, 4, 5, 36, 56
Leblond, Alexander, architect, 16, 23
Lenin, 2, 10, 47, 50, 52, 53, 54
Leningrad, characteristics, 1-4, 59-61
  climate, 20
  cultural importance, 70-2
  industry, 65
  modern architecture, 65-6
  Moscow compared, 59
Lermontov, Mikhail, 33
Leskov, Nikolay, 40
Lissitsky, 65
Lomonosov, Mikhail, 27, 28
Lunacharsky, Anatoli, 64

Malevitch, Kasimir, 65
Mamontov, 44
Marble Palace, 30, 64
Marinsky Theatre, 1, 44, 74
Mars Field, 64
Marxist Movement, 47
Mattarnovy, Georg, architect, 16
Mayakovsky, Vladimir, 55
Medtner, Nikolai, 50
Mendeleyev, Dmitri, 2, 32, 69
Mensheviks, 10, 47, 48
Menshikov, Aleksandr, 10
Meyerhold, Vsevolod, 38, 51
Mikhailov Palace, 34
Moika Canal, 22, 64, 70, 73

Molotov, Vyacheslav, 51
Montferrand, August, archi-
    tect, 35
Morozov, Ivan, 44
Moscow, 18, 19, 44, 56
Moussorgsky, Modest, 38, 44
Muscovy, 11

Narva, 4, 7
Nekrasov, 69
Neva, 4, 5, 6, 9, 10, 35, 68
Nevsky Prospect, 1, 3, 9, 20,
    22, 35–6, 57, 64, 67
Nicholas I, 37, 39, 40, 41
    statue, 67
Nicholas II, 42, 46, 48, 49, 51
Nijinsky, Vaslav, 51
Nikolsky, A. S., architect, 66
Novgorod, 4
Nyenskans, 6

Oblomov, 41, 45
Okhta, river, 6
Orthodox Church, 6, 7, 19

Palmyra, 4
Paul I, 37, 38
Pavlov, Ivan, 33
Pavlova, Anna, 1, 51
Pavlovsk, 30
Peter the Great, 4–14
    capital proclaimed, 10
    character, 13–14
    city founded, 6
    Emperor, 11
    first home, 9
    foreigners encouraged, 5, 13
    reforms, 12

and State Church, 7
    statue, 67
    wars, 4–7
    Westernization, 11
Peter II, 18
Peter III, 18, 25
Peterhof, 22–3
Petipa, Marius, 38
Petrashevsky, M. V., 39–40
Petrograd, 2, 15, 52
Petrokrepost, 5
Plekhanov, Georgii, 47
Poltava, 7
Popov, A. A., scientist, 69
Porcelain, 28
Potemkin, Grigorii, 26, 30
Poverty, 43–4
Prokofiev, Sergei, 50
Purges, 50, 61–2
Pushkin, Aleksandr, 2, 32, 33,
    72–3

Quarenghi, Giacomo, archi-
    tect, 26, 29

Rachmaninov, Sergei, 50–1
Radishchev, Alexander, 27
Rasputin, 29, 51
Rastrelli, Bartolomeo, archi-
    tect, 21–3, 25
Repin, Ilya, painter, 50
Revolution, March, 52–3
    November, 54
Revolutionary movements, 45,
    47–8
Rimsky-Korsakov, Nikolai, 44
Rinaldi, A., architect, 26, 30

Roerich, N. C. artist, 50
Rossi, C. I., architect, 34

St Isaac's Cathedral, 35, 48
SS Peter and Paul, fortress and
      cathedral, 6, 7, 17, 57
St Petersburg, buildings, 8–9
      industrialization, 42–3
      name, 15
      population, 19
      trade, 19, 25, 28
Saltykov-Shchedrin,   Mikhail,
      writer, 40
Saltykov-Shchedrin Library, 73
Schlüsselburg, 5
Science, 32–3
Scriabin, Alexander, 50–1
Shostakovitch, Dimitri, 57
Siege (2nd World War), 56–7
Smolny, 22, 30, 54
Social Democrats, 42, 47
Social Revolutionaries, 45, 52
Socialist Realism, 55
Soil Science, 32–3
Soviets, 48, 53
      1st Congress, 10
Stalin, (Iosif) ,55, 56, 57, 61, 65
Starov, architect, 30
Stolypin, Petr, 51
Stravinsky, Igor, 37, 50
Streltsy, 13
Summer Palace, 10, 16
Sweden, wars with, 4

Tatlin, V., artist, 65
Tavrida Palace, 30, 49
Tchaikovsky, Peter, 2, 38, 73

Terem, 11, 13, 16
Third Section (secret police), 32
Thomas de Thomon, architect,
      35
Tolstoy, Leo, 44
Tovstonogov, theatre director,
      74
Trezzini, G. A., architect, 6, 10
Trotsky, Leon, 48, 54, 55
Tsarskoe Selo, 22, 23, 25, 29
Turgenev, Ivan, 33, 38, 41, 69

University, 16, 69–70

Vallin de la Motte, architect,
      26, 29
Vasilievsky Ostrov, 9, 10, 35
Vavilov, N. I., geneticist, 57
Voronikhin, A. N., architect,
      35
Vyborg Side, 9

War, Civil, 55
      First World, 51–2
      Second World, 56
Winter Palace, 22
Workers' movements, 31, 46

Yablochkov, P. M., scientist, 33
Yesenin, Sergey, 55
Yusupov Palace, 29

Zakharov, A. D., architect, 34
Zemstvo, 41
Zhdanov, Andrei, 62
Zhuk, architect, 66